WHEN LIFE IS
HARD

Turning Your Trials to Gold

JAMES
MACDONALD

LifeWay Press®
Nashville, Tennessee

Published by LifeWay Press®
© 2010 James MacDonald
Second printing 2011

ISBN 978-1-4158-6925-3
Item 005293072

Dewey decimal classification: 248.84
Subject headings: CHRISTIAN LIFE \ JOY AND SORROW \ SUFFERING

To order additional copies of this resource, write to LifeWay Church Resources Customer Service; One LifeWay Plaza; Nashville, TN 37234-0113; fax (615) 251-5933; phone toll free (800) 458-2772; e-mail orderentry@lifeway.com; order online at www.lifeway.com; or visit a LifeWay Christian Store.

Printed in the United States of America

Leadership and Adult Publishing
LifeWay Church Resources
One LifeWay Plaza
Nashville, TN 37234-0175

CONTENTS

THE AUTHOR

James MacDonald is the founding and senior pastor of Harvest Bible Chapel in the northwestern suburbs of Chicago, Illinois. Harvest Bible Chapel is a church based on prayer, boldness in evangelism, Spirit-filled worship, and the unapologetic proclamation of God's Word. In its first 18 years Harvest has grown to more than 10,000 members. Additionally, it has sent out more than 1,000 leaders to launch 15 new churches with more than 8,000 in attendance.

James's teaching can be heard on the daily, 30-minute radio program *Walk in the Word*, which airs across North America. The mission of *Walk in the Word* is to ignite passion in God's people through the proclamation of biblical truth.

Born in London, Ontario, Canada, James received his master's degree from Trinity Evangelical Divinity School in Deerfield, Illinois, and his doctorate from Phoenix Seminary. He and his wife, Kathy, have three children and reside in Chicago.

For more information about James and these ministries, visit *www.harvestbible.org* or *www.walkintheword.com*.

Other Books by James MacDonald

Always True: God's Promises When Life Is Hard small-group study (LifeWay Press, 2011)
Always True: God's Five Promises for When Life Is Hard (Moody Publishers, 2011)
Ancient Wisdom (B&H Publishing Group, 2006)
Downpour: He Will Come to Us like the Rain small-group study (LifeWay Press, 2006)
Downpour: He Will Come to Us like the Rain (B&H Publishing Group, 2006)
God Wrote a Book (Crossway Books, 2002)
Gripped by the Greatness of God small-group study (LifeWay Press, 2005)
Gripped by the Greatness of God (Moody Publishers, 2005)
I Really Want to Change . . . So, Help Me God (Moody Publishers, 2000)
Lord, Change My Attitude small-group study (LifeWay Press, 2008)
Lord, Change My Attitude . . . Before It's Too Late (Moody Publishers, 2001)
Seven Words to Change Your Family (Moody Publishers, 2001)
When Life Is Hard (Moody Publishers, 2010)

Visit *www.lifeway.com/jamesmacdonald* for information about James MacDonald resources published by LifeWay.

PREFACE

Maybe you noticed that I titled this study *When Life Is Hard*, not *If Life Is Hard*. I have found that real living isn't an easy existence occasionally ruffled by difficulty. Authentic, on-the-edge-of-your-seat living is made up of trials and hardship, occasionally interrupted by amazing relief. Most believers realize it's always possible to find others who are having harder times, but I haven't met any committed Christians who are having easy lives. Life is a challenge. Yet the Christian life is a purposeful challenge.

If you picked up this workbook with the mistaken expectation that it would help you discover a way to make life easy, you will be greatly disappointed. Here's the truth: nothing in this study is going to make life easier. People may face varying degrees of hardship; but let me warn you that the vibrant, in-touch life God has for us as Christians was never designed to be easy.

In the winter of 2008–9 I traveled to California for cancer treatments. A lot happened before that trip, during that trip, and after that trip to teach me what Christians face when they suffer. This study is not really my story, but I will use parts of my story to illustrate just how *hard* hard times can be. My difficulties and challenges are not the worst I've ever heard about by a long shot, but through these trials God taught me how to understand, cope with, and benefit from hard times.

As we begin this study, I don't know exactly what trials you are going through; but your Heavenly Father does! In the weeks to come, you will have many opportunities to learn what the Bible says about trials, why God allows them, and what He wants to teach you through them. Make sure you listen attentively to what He has to say to you. Let's dive together into our study of *When Life Is Hard*.

How to Get the Most from This Study

1. **Attend each group experience.**
   - Watch the DVD teaching.
   - Participate in the group discussion.
2. **Complete the daily assignments in this workbook.**
   - Read the material.
   - Complete the learning activities.
   - Watch for God to change your conduct and your character as He works for your good through your trial.

WHAT ARE TRIALS?

This Week's Scripture Focus

"Have you forgotten the exhortation that addresses you as sons?

'My son, do not regard lightly the discipline of the Lord,
  nor be weary when reproved by him.
For the Lord disciplines the one he loves,
  and chastises every son whom he receives.'

"It is for discipline that you have to endure. God is treating you as sons. For what son is there whom his father does not discipline? If you are left without discipline, in which all have participated, then you are illegitimate children and not sons. Besides this, we have had earthly fathers who disciplined us and we respected them. Shall we not much more be subject to the Father of spirits and live? For they disciplined us for a short time as it seemed best to them, but he disciplines us for our good, that we may share his holiness. For the moment all discipline seems painful rather than pleasant, but later it yields the peaceful fruit of righteousness to those who have been trained by it." *Hebrews 12:5-11*

In Training for Life

Hard times, discipline, trials—who does a study about these things? Well, we are about to do just that. The hard times that happen in life are usually not experiences we sign up for or look forward to, but they happen anyway. So we need to start figuring out why they happen, what good can come from them, and how to respond to them.

Think about the training experiences you have had throughout your life. Training is a form of trial. The purpose of training, however, is usually announced in advance. If you enlisted in the military, you knew there would be training. Basic training was part of the conversation when you signed your life away. But hearing about training is quite different from having a drill sergeant wake you up at four in the morning for some fun activities. Nevertheless, you expect training even if it turns out to be harder than you thought it would be.

If you've ever hired a personal trainer, you know the main thing you are paying for is their willingness to be obnoxious with you. Once you've committed to a certain routine, they are going to keep you at it even when and especially when you come up with a good excuse not to follow through on your commitment!

Personal training and military training, as difficult as they might be, can't hold a candle to the relentlessness of God's discipline. Maybe you didn't expect this training when you became a believer. But the reality is if God is in your life, He is coming hard toward you with continuous, lifelong, loving discipline. So this week we will explore the nature of these trials that God wants to use in our lives.

GROUP EXPERIENCE

As You Gather

1. If you are meeting as a group for the first time, take a moment for personal introductions.

2. Share an experience when you received training or when you trained someone else. What did you learn about training?

3. In what ways has training been particularly beneficial in your life?

Preparation and Review

1. What are examples of situations that could be called hard times in life?

2. When did a hard time you experienced in the past produce good results that you now recognize?

DVD Session 1 Viewer Guide

1. Trials are extremely _difficult_.

2. There are many _kinds_ of trials.

3. _____ encounters trials.

   A trial is a _____ circumstance allowed by God
   to change my _conduct_ and my _character_.

4. Everyone is going through a trial _in God's family_

5. There are many terms for trials in the **New Testament**, including *suffering, hardship, difficulty, chastening,* and _discipline_.

1. What is the discipline of the Lord?

   Our acknowledging that we don't have the _strength_ needed
   to see us through the Lord's discipline is exactly what God is going for.

2. Why does the Lord discipline His children?

The way out of a consequence is _repentance_.

He disciplines us because He _loves_ us.

3. How should I respond to the Lord's discipline?

We must _say_, "You are right, God."
We must _submit_ to God.

4. What results from the Lord's discipline?

When God disciplines us, He has a good _purpose_ in mind.

God's purposes in our discipline are very _good_—not at all
like Satan, who continuously condemns us with _____.

faith is the absence of everything that causes turmoil,
pain, restlessness, and fear.

5. How do I make the most from the Lord's discipline?

The _trial_ is momentary.
The _Benefit_ is immense.
The _____ is conditional.

Responding to the DVD Teaching

1. **How would you answer in your own words, What are trials?**

2. **What questions about trials do you hope will be answered in this study?**

3. **What is the difference between consequences of our actions and hard times that seem to come out of nowhere? Identify examples of both.**

4. **Describe one way you have submitted to training from the Lord. What happened after you responded that way?**

Read week 1 and complete the activities before the next group experience.

Day 1

RECOGNIZING TRIALS

Today's Scripture Focus

"Have you forgotten the exhortation that addresses you as sons?
'My son, do not regard lightly the discipline of the Lord,
nor be weary when reproved by him.' "

Hebrews 12:5

Jesus knew what it was like to be treated as a son under discipline. He knew what it was like to face a distasteful, difficult circumstance with no immediate way out. There was only one way *through:* by submitting to God's will. That's why, in the garden of Gethsemane, Jesus could pray about the cup passing from Him yet later accept that the suffering before Him was the very cup His Father had prepared for Him. Knowing that this was the Father's will wouldn't make the trial easier, but Jesus knew He could trust His Father.

In the same way, our knowing what trials are won't transform something hard into something easy. By the time we have gone through these six weeks of study, I can guarantee you will still have questions, and you will still struggle when you encounter hard times in the future. But beyond all of the questions and answers, I pray that you will emerge from this study with a deepened and settled trust in God. Truly knowing God as He wants to be known is even better than having answers. And trusting Him makes the answers we have go a lot further!

> A trial is a painful circumstance allowed by God to change our conduct and our character.

Defining a Trial

Throughout this study we will use this definition of *trial:* a trial is a painful circumstance allowed by God to change our conduct and our character.

That definition includes four components that allow us to regard any circumstance in our lives as a potential trial. What are they?

1. painful
2. no control
3. forces change
4. teaches

Based on your personal experience and observations and keeping in mind the characteristics of a trial, add at least one more example of each type of trial below.

Small trial: flat tire; _things that break_

Large trial: broken leg; _car wreck_

Short trial: flight delay; _____

Long trial: canceled flight; _weight_

Irritating trial: headache; _back goes out_

Devastating trial: cancer diagnosis; _____

Stretching trial: child leaving home; _retirement_

Devastating trial: losing a child; _child with cancer_

All of us in God's family are experiencing one or more trials now. Identify current circumstances in your life that seem to fit the description of a trial.

Job is the biblical character most commonly associated with suffering. Over the course of a few days, Job endured more suffering than most people do in a lifetime, losing his children, his wealth, and his health. The striking thing about Job is the way he endured his trial. Have you ever heard of the patience of Job? He earned that reputation by maintaining his faith in God throughout his ordeal. Job summarized his position like this:

> "He [God] knows the way that I take;
> when he has tried me, I shall come out as gold." *Job 23:10*

Job acknowledged that God allowed his trial; yet Job submitted to the process and expressed confidence that God would bring positive change from his suffering. Job's words epitomize the hopeful view of trials we are going for in this study. Trials come to all of us; but if we respond with faith, God will bring us out of the experience as gold.

> Job expressed confidence that God would bring positive change from his suffering.

The Lord's Discipline

The Bible frequently uses the word *discipline* for *trial;* for example, the word *discipline* is central to Hebrews 12:5, our focal Scripture today. What is "the discipline of the Lord"?

Read the following passages and record the synonyms for *discipline*.

"I am sure of this, that he who began a good work in you
will bring it to completion at the day of Jesus Christ." *Philippians 1:6*

***Discipline* is equated with** *teaching* .

"Count it all joy, my brothers, when you meet trials of various kinds,
for you know that the testing of your faith produces steadfastness."
James 1:2-3

***Discipline* means** _____ **and** _____.

"The grace of God has appeared, bringing salvation for all people,
training us to renounce ungodliness and worldly passions, and to live
self-controlled, upright, and godly lives in the present age." *Titus 2:11-12*

***Discipline* means** _____.

Hebrews 12:5 says not to be weary when we are reproved by God. *Reproof* is still
another synonym for *trial*.

Read 2 Timothy 3:16-17:

"All Scripture is breathed out by God and profitable for teaching,
for reproof, for correction, and for training in righteousness,
that the man of God may be competent, equipped for every good work."

In what ways is the Bible our guidebook for discipline or reproof?

God allows challenging circumstances in our lives for a reason.

Hebrews 12:5 teaches that discipline is "of the Lord," and our definition of *trial*
states that a trial is allowed by God. It's important for Christians to remember
that God allows challenging circumstances in our lives for a reason. Our job is to
trust Him and learn what He wants to do in and through us.

Hebrews 12:5 reminds us to avoid two negative responses to the Lord's work of
discipline in our lives: regarding it lightly and becoming weary.

What do you think it means to regard lightly the discipline of the Lord?

What do you think it means to become weary under God's disciplining hand?

When you consider the Lord's disciplining work in your life, are you more likely to regard it lightly or become weary with God's methods?

Poor in Spirit

So the writer of Hebrews is telling us that if you're a follower of Christ, discipline is coming. Testing is coming. Reproof is coming. It's one of the more sobering aspects of the Christian life that's likely to leave you feeling vulnerable.

Have you ever bounced a check? If so, you were either caught by surprise and shocked to discover you didn't have as much in your account as you thought, or you were ashamed because you had assumed you could cover the check before it cleared the bank. To make matters worse, you were assessed a monetary penalty for your indiscretion. The feeling of indebtedness or temporary bankruptcy isn't pleasant. The fact that your check was denied is a harsh slap of reality.

The same thing can occur in other areas of life. How often do you balance your ethical accounts? How much do you have in your goodwill-toward-others account? What was the last withdrawal you made from your spiritual-gifts fund? There's nothing like the demands of God's discipline to show us how little we have in our accounts.

One purpose of discipline is that God wants us to be aware of our utter dependence on Him. This is true from the beginning to the end of our experience with God in this life. In the Beatitudes Jesus described the basic building blocks

God wants us to be aware of our utter dependence on Him.

As uncomfortable as helplessness may be, it's what God is going for when He disciplines us.

of a relationship with God. His first instruction was "Blessed are the poor in spirit, for theirs is the kingdom of heaven" (Matt. 5:3). "Poor in spirit" means spiritually bankrupt—nothing to bring to the table, no resources to cash in. We come to God empty-handed. And from that point on, anything we have is what our Heavenly Father has given to us. As uncomfortable as helplessness may be, it's what God is going for when He disciplines us. It's not that He enjoys our being helpless; rather, He knows unless we realize our helplessness, we won't rely on Him or experience all He has for us and all He can accomplish through us. You see, God really knows what He's doing!

Think about a trial you are going through. Check the statement that best expresses the way you are responding.

☐ **I am responding with scorn.**

☐ **I am responding with weariness.**

☐ **I am submitting to God and learning what He wants to teach me.**

☐ **Other:**

No matter how you are responding to God's discipline, write a prayer expressing your thoughts to God, admitting your helplessness, and describing the way you want to respond to His discipline in the future.

How do your past experiences show that God really knows what He's doing when He disciplines you?

Day 2

WHY DOES THE LORD DISCIPLINE HIS CHILDREN?

Today's Scripture Focus

" 'The Lord disciplines the one he loves, and chastises every son whom he receives.' It is for discipline that you have to endure. God is treating you as sons. For what son is there whom his father does not discipline? If you are left without discipline, in which all have participated, then you are illegitimate children and not sons."

Hebrews 12:6-8

Does God spank His children? Yes, He does! This fact is stated in Hebrews 12:6, part of today's key passage, which quotes Proverbs 3:12. The phrase "chastises every son whom he receives" means our Heavenly Father doles out loving punishment to His children when that is necessary. One way He does this is by letting the consequences of sin take their course in our lives. This concept flies directly in the face of the modern, watered-down image of God as a kindly soul who wouldn't hurt a fly. I sometimes wonder how often God has to discipline people who angrily inform Him that if He dares punish them for the deliberate disobedience they are about commit, well, they won't *like* Him anymore.

Threatening God with unbelief or a cold shoulder is about as effective as the tactic we used with our parents when we threatened to hold our breath until we got our way. I don't know about your dad, but mine saw tricks like that coming a mile away, and he didn't hesitate to chastise me when I needed it. And even when his punishment caused discomfort, I knew his love for me as my father ultimately motivated this discipline.

Does God spank His children?

Proof of Love

So why does the Lord discipline you?

Because he love you

How does today's focal Scripture answer that question?

It says he chastises every son

Hebrews 12:6 says, "The Lord disciplines the one he loves." Well, there you go. God disciplines you because He loves you. Far from folding His arms, God rolls up His sleeves to get ready to do something good in your life. Far from abandoning you when you go through difficult trials, God moves toward you. Isn't that good news? In fact, trials are proofs of love.

Never forget this: if God allows your life to become hard, His motivation is always love. He *loves* you. His eyes are on you. His attention is directed toward you. All of His thoughts are about you. The goal of all your pain is your restoration to a deeper sense of His love. But keep in mind that this is biblical love—a love that is willing to take you through a valley to get you to a hilltop. No pseudosolutions or quick fixes with God. He is going for change in you at the deepest and most lasting level.

Think about your trial. What feelings are you experiencing in dealing with it?

☐ **Fear**　　☐ **Abandonment**　　☐ **Loneliness**　　☐ **Confidence**

☐ **Anger**　　☐ **Hopelessness**　　☐ **Hopefulness**　　☐ **Comfort**

☐ **Other:** *all of the above*

What evidence of God's love have you seen in your situation?

he gives me strength

Mark Twain's book *Tom Sawyer* reflects a profound understanding of the connection between love and discipline. Twain was a keen observer of human nature. The scene in which Aunt Polly is making life hard for Tom Sawyer while Huck Finn laughs from his hiding place is a classic portrayal of human reactions. We tend to smile when others are being disciplined, especially if we are just as guilty of wrongdoing. We're just happy we didn't get caught. But later Huck Finn weeps when he realizes no one in his life cares enough about him to guide, discipline, and even punish him. He realizes firsthand that pain can be a reminder that someone really loves us.

Identify a past experience when you know God's discipline and training showed His love for you.

the death of my son

I once heard a child-development expert say on television, "No good could ever come from causing a child pain." I couldn't disagree more! The statement is nonsense. It automatically places the following things in the bad category: birth, shots, dentists, spankings, and any parental response (such as saying no) that causes a child to cry.

In a typical loving parent-child relationship, how would you categorize the following? Use _D_ for _discipline_, _P_ for _punishment for wrongdoing_, and _U_ for _undetermined_.

_D_ **Encouraging you to walk when you still wanted to crawl even though you would sometimes fall**

_D_ **Giving you a regular chore like loading the dishwasher**

_D_ **Spanking you for lying**

_D_ **Insisting that you put borrowed tools back in place though it was inconvenient**

_D_ **Holding you to a promise you made**

_P_ **Making you pay for a window you broke**

_P_ **Withholding driving privileges from you even though you were going to pay the fine for your speeding ticket**

_D_ **Taking you to the dentist even though you were afraid of drills**

What are some good things that have come from painful experiences in your life?

empathy
stronger faith

Scriptures like Romans 8:32 point to Jesus' painful death on the cross as the source of good things for believers:

> "He who did not spare his own Son but gave him up for us all,
> how will he not also with him graciously give us all things?"

List some of the good things in your life that resulted from the cross of Christ.

the certainty of heaven
never alone

Consequence or Trial?

Take a close look at your situation, because the way forward is different if your hardship is a consequence of sin rather than a trial. A consequence is the direct result of sin you have committed. The way out of a consequence is repentance. If you did something wrong, you need to make it right with God through repentance and with the people your sin injured through restitution. A trial is a completely different scenario. You didn't bring a trial into your life. Remember, a trial is a painful circumstance allowed by God to transform your conduct and your character. God Himself allowed that into your life.

A consequence is the direct result of sin you have committed.

If you are going through a trial, is it a consequence of sin or God's discipline?

What clues helped you distinguish between the two?

The way out of a consequence is repentance. If your hardship is the result of wrongdoing on your part, take a moment to repent and confess it to God. Ask for His forgiveness and for His help in overcoming the consequences of your actions. Is there anyone to whom you need to apologize and make restitution? If so, plan to do this.

Are You Being Disciplined?

One of today's verses says, "God is treating you as sons" (v. 7). So if you're reading this verse and thinking, *All this talk about trials is interesting; but everything's rocking in my house, and it's been like that for a long time. No real problems of any kind. I'm in great health, and everything's great with my family.* I hate to tell you, but that's not good news for you. All of God's kids are receiving discipline. If you have no trials in your life at all, you need to go back and ask yourself whether you are part of God's family through faith in Christ. The possibility that you are not in the family may shock you, but you can repent and allow God to make you His child.

How do you know you are in God's family?

I believe in Jesus - give my life to him

Now read these verses:

> "To all who did receive him, who believed in his name,
> he gave the right to become children of God." *John 1:12*

> "God gave us eternal life, and this life is in his Son. Whoever has the Son
> has life; whoever does not have the Son of God does not have life."
> *1 John 5:11-12*

Does your answer to the previous question match God's criteria in these verses? *yes*

John 1:12 says the only people who have the authority to be God's children are those who have received Jesus. I hope you've made that life-changing decision.

Hebrews 12:8 explains, "If you are left without discipline, in which all have participated, then you are illegitimate." If you're not getting the discipline "in which all have participated," you need to take a closer look at your heart and your hope.

Maybe you're thinking, *As much as I appreciate this proof of sonship, sometimes I wish I didn't have this stuff going on in my life.* Yes, I understand. Honestly, at times things seemed easier before we came to Christ. In a sense they were.

But in another sense they were not. You were so clueless then. You didn't get the whole picture. You had no idea where you were going. You didn't know the big answers for anything or what God is all about. There's no question that the sons of this world have it easier for about the next 10 minutes! But then, if they don't come to faith in Christ, it *really* goes downhill after that. What a sad and tragic end awaits those who reject Christ—God's only provision for their salvation. What a glorious thing to be called a son or a daughter of the living God through faith in Jesus Christ.

Part of being in the family means God is now working on you. One reason we have difficulty accepting His work in our lives is that our view of Him is so limited. God is much greater than we give Him credit for. He really knows what He's doing, so we can trust Him when hardship comes our way. When you're in the mist of trials, you can rejoice to know that God loves you and that He will work in your circumstances according to His larger purposes for your life. He is molding you into what He wants you to be for eternity. So determine now to get the full benefit from your trials. Life is short, and eternity is very, very long.

God is much greater than we give Him credit for.

Explain in your own words how God's discipline proves His love for His children.

What clues do you have, if any, about what God may be doing through a current trial you are experiencing?

If you have doubts that you are part of God's family, talk to God about this. Seek the guidance of your pastor or another mature believer.

If you know you are God's child, commit your trial to your Father and ask Him to show you His love through this time of discipline and to help you learn what He intends for you.

Day 3

WHEN THE GOING GETS TOUGH

Today's Scripture Focus

"Besides this, we have had earthly fathers who disciplined us
and we respected them. Shall we not much more
be subject to the Father of spirits and live?"

Hebrews 12:9

Each of us is living history. The fact that you can read these words means that you have gone through a process of education. Can you remember learning to read? Do you recall the halting efforts to sound out words and the wonder of realizing that the sounds of the letters worked together to form words, sentences, and meaning? All of that took time; someone didn't let you give up.

You also had to learn to walk. At first you fell down a lot. You may still have the scars to prove it! You may not remember the sense of freedom you had the first time you walked across the room into the arms of a waiting parent, but it must have kept you going. Others offered encouragement. You went from a tumbling toddler to a confident walker. Later, you learned to walk and chew gum at the same time!

These steps of development prepared us for the next lessons in life. That's why the writer of Hebrews could say, "We have had earthly fathers" and expect to make a point. He was appealing to his readers' living history. Today's verse says your earthly father disciplined you, and you respected him for it. When it comes to discipline, we can get clues from our past experiences, good or bad.

> **When it comes to discipline, we can get clues from our past experiences.**

Think for a moment about your father, teachers, and other influential persons who reared you. Identify three of them and describe their positive contributions to your life.

_____Mother_____ **taught me by ...** *example*

As a result, I ... *learned to walk in faith*

_____ taught me by ...

As a result, I ...

_____ taught me by ...

As a result, I ...

In what ways have you respected or acknowledged those "fathers" recently? How could you express your gratitude for the benefits they gave you?

Fathers of Faith

This week's Scripture focus, Hebrews 12:5-11, has an important history and context for a discussion of godly influences. Do you remember the subject of the preceding chapter of Hebrews? Turn to Hebrews 11 and look at the paragraph headings in your Bible. Run your finger down the page and observe the names that pop out at you—Abel, Noah, Abraham, Sarah, Moses, and so on. They were all included in the chapter for one reason.

If Hebrews 12:5-11 is all about _discipline_, Hebrews 11 is all about _____.

When people look back on your life, will they mention faith and discipline in describing your time on earth? Why?

Hard times in your life can be teachable moments that God uses to grow your faith.

One of my prayers for this study is that you will have a much clearer perspective on the way hard times in your life can be teachable moments that God uses to grow your faith.

Hebrews 11 has long been recognized as the hall of biblical heroes, our ancient fathers of faith. They are what Hebrews 12:1 calls a "cloud of witnesses" because their lives offer us countless examples of faith and life lessons in what it means to walk with God. So when the writer says, "We have had earthly fathers who disciplined us and we respected them" (Heb. 12:9), he has our immediate biological dads in mind; but the context reminds us that we've got a huge crowd of examples we can't ignore, sort of looking down on us from history.

But don't miss the passage that comes immediately before Hebrews 12:5-11. Verses 2-4 focus on the role Jesus plays as the "founder and perfecter of our faith" (v. 2). He is the source and object of our faith because He "endured the cross, despising the shame" (v. 2).

Read Hebrews 12:2:

> ". . . looking to Jesus, the founder and perfecter of our faith, who for the joy that was set before him endured the cross, despising the shame, and is seated at the right hand of the throne of God."

In the sense that we have been using the term *discipline* in this study, how would you describe the cross of Jesus as discipline in His life?

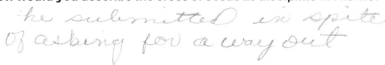
he submitted in spite of asking for a way out

According to Hebrews 12:3, as we struggle in our lives, we always ought to "consider him who endured." Jesus is our number one reason not to "grow weary or fainthearted" along the way, because we have His example and because we have His empowering presence in our lives.

Yet even with the array of biblical examples and Jesus' ultimate example to draw on, the writer still tells us to remember our imperfect human fathers and appreciate their flawed efforts to discipline us. In one way or another, they turned us around. Their training got our attention. And we respected them for it. We can bring that perspective to the hard experiences God allows in our lives.

Jesus is our number one reason not to "grow weary or fainthearted."

How Should I Respond to God's Discipline?

The examples in our lives—our earthly fathers and spiritual fathers—require two responses from us that we can find in Hebrews 12:9.

1. We have to admit we have a problem or an area in our lives that requires discipline and training.

2. We have to submit to the discipline God provides.

One reason we don't like hard times is that they expose problems, weaknesses, and blindness. Not only do we dislike the experiences themselves, but we also resist what they point out in us. That's why we instinctively use three levels of defense against admitting that God has put His finger of discipline on a place in us that needs it:

1. Denial

2. Deflection

3. Excuse or explanation

Read the following expressions that illustrate these defensive responses toward God during hard times. Beside each statement write the number from the previous list that corresponds to the response that is expressed.

_1_ **This may be a hard time, but it has nothing to teach me.**

_2_ **I can see that these difficulties are revealing weaknesses in me, but they are not my fault! Someone else is responsible.**

_1_ **Problems? What problems? I don't need these trials!**

_3_ **Look, there may a problem here, but it belongs to someone else. I'm just caught up in the backwash from my wife's/kid's/friend's problems. Things will be better when they get straightened out!**

_2_ **I realize I've got this problem, but I inherited it. Look at my dad; he's the same way. I can't help it.**

_2_ **I don't understand why God is letting me go through this trial. Several people in my small group could really learn from hard times like these!**

We have to admit we have a problem that requires discipline.

Until we get beyond these defenses against the discipline of the Lord, the good results that can come from our difficult experience won't arrive. We have to admit we have a problem that requires discipline.

So how do we put these defenses in our rearview mirror? Notice the last phrase in Hebrews 12:9: "Shall we not much more be subject to the Father of spirits and live?" "Be subject" means *submit*—our second response to God's discipline. Admittedly, submission is not a hot-button idea in society today. The world's mind-set is contrasubmission. But the verse says to submit ("be subject") to the "Father of spirits," to God Himself.

James 4:7 highlights an important reason we need to submit to God during a trial: "Submit yourselves therefore to God. Resist the devil, and he will flee from you." If you're going through a hard time, the Devil is always standing by, ready to point out that God doesn't care and isn't going to take care of you. Effective resistance to the Devil always begins with submission to God. We can't resist in our own strength and expect the Devil to be impressed or motivated to flee. But aligning ourselves with God through submission allows us to rest in the truth that God's ways are best, and the Devil has to come through God to get at us.

Effective resistance to the Devil always begins with submission to God.

What difference do you think it would make if you always responded to Satan's attacks by immediately declaring your submission to God?

trials would be shorter

If you are experiencing a trial, can you honestly say you have submitted it to God?

If not, why?

☐ **Lack of trust**

☐ **Didn't see it as God's discipline**

☐ **Blamed God**

☐ **Didn't admit the problem**

☐ **Other:**

Before we can begin to see the good results that God intends to develop through discipline, we have to engage those areas of discipline as fully as we can. It's not easy to pray, "Do it now, Lord. Cut deep. Get it all. I'm leaning into what You have placed before me. Accomplish all that You intend in me through this trial." But that prayer can be an effective expression of submission that will free you to learn from the trial your Heavenly Father has allowed in your life.

Pray about the issue of submitting your trial to God. You may need to repent of wrong ideas, anger, or blame. Try to submit to His will in this circumstance.

Day 4
THE BIG TAKEAWAY

Today's Scripture Focus

"They disciplined us for a short time as it seemed best to them, but he disciplines us for our good, that we may share his holiness."

Hebrews 12:10

Every year thousands of people wonder what it would be like to stand at the top of the world, the peak of Mount Everest. Hundreds of people make the trek to at least look at the mountain. Each climbing season dozens of adventurers manage to arrive at one of the base camps around the grandest of all mountains. But the schizophrenic weather, the difficult climbing, and the extreme heights winnow climbers on the mountain to a hardy handful. Few make it to the top. Some even die trying.

Meanwhile, millions of others don't get it. They shake their heads, perplexed. Why on earth would anyone in their right mind go to such extremes and have nothing to show for it afterward? Why risk so much for such a small reward? We want our successes to come with tangible results. There's not a trophy waiting at the summit of the mountain, so why even climb in the first place? When asked that question, English mountaineer George Leigh Mallory is credited with the famous statement "Because it's there."[1] Is that it? Climbers are driven to climb whatever is in front of them?

Or is the result something more subtle? Is the takeaway something unseen but precious? Climbers may come back from the summit empty-handed, but that doesn't mean they descend with nothing. The test of the climb and the effort to reach the top have brought out something in them and taught them about themselves. The trial has changed them. The climb has disciplined them. Those who never climb have a hard time imagining the value of results like these.

Which of the following activities offer you a challenge that is itself the reward?

☐ **Running**

☑ **Practicing an interpersonal skill like listening**

☑ **Participating in a group Bible study**

☑ **Following through on a task**

- ☐ **Staying in touch with old friends**
- ☒ **Practicing a daily devotional habit**
- ☐ **Memorizing and meditating on Scripture**
- ☐ **Other:**

Why are these activities so rewarding for you?

Sharing His Holiness

Today's Scripture focus reminds us that God's discipline comes with a reward. Through our trial our Heavenly Father is disciplining us for our good—to make us holy. When people read this truth, they often admit they were expecting more from God as a result of the hard times in life. They say, "Holiness? For my good? That's really it? The takeaway is something I become, not something I get?" And the only appropriate answer is a resounding yes!

Why the letdown? Because our expectations tend to be almost the exact opposite of God's intentions. First, we don't readily connect hardness and goodness. We hesitate to believe something difficult can be good for us. We have mixed feelings when we memorize verses like Romans 8:28: "We know that for those who love God all things work together for good, for those who are called according to his purpose." "All things" must necessarily include hard things. But we have a difficult time getting our minds around the idea that when God is at work, even hard things can bring good into our lives.

Second, we tend to be clueless about holiness. A. W. Tozer wrote, "Neither the writer nor the reader of these words is qualified to appreciate the holiness of God. Quite literally a new channel must be cut through the desert of our minds to allow the sweet waters that will heal our great sickness to flow in."[2] What exactly does it mean to be holy, anyway?

What is your personal definition of *holiness?* If we agree that God is holy, in what sense can we be holy?

God's discipline comes with a reward.

What do the following verses tell you about holiness? Write what each verse says about holiness or sanctification (the process of becoming holy).

Exodus 3:4-5:

Exodus 20:8-11:

Ephesians 1:3-4:

Ephesians 2:19-22:

Ephesians 4:22-24:

Colossians 1:21-23:

1 Thessalonians 4:7:

1 Peter 1:13-16:

Now write a new definition of *holiness*, based on these passages.

God hardwired us to desire holiness.

Hebrews 12:10 makes it clear that our holiness is God's ultimate objective for each of us, and discipline is His method. Our parents give us their best shot in a limited way for a short time, but God is in it for the long haul. The longing for something deep and meaningful that saturates our every pursuit reveals that God hardwired us to desire holiness—authentic connection with Him. The phrase "that we may share his holiness" describes the source of holiness—God Himself. So if you are a child of God through faith in Christ, your Father will use His loving discipline to make you holy.

For Our Good

Consider this: the people around you are in one way or another pursuing holiness. If they aren't following God, they pursue an infinite number of substitutes for what we were designed to desire. They may risk everything for wealth, pleasure, or power, believing that achieving any of these things will result in the wholeness they long for. But they are deceived. They arrive at destinations that were advertised to give them fulfillment only to discover emptiness. Instead of wholeness, they find a vacuum in their lives that still hasn't been filled because it can be received only through a relationship with God.

Identify something you once pursued that didn't satisfy.

Why is the pursuit of holiness the only thing that can satisfy our most basic longings?

What a tragedy it is when we who claim to be children of God fail to admit we desperately need to grow in holiness or to submit to God's Fatherly discipline. How could His training fail to result in good for us when it flows from His love for us? And what could be better than to discover over a lifetime that He has disciplined us into holiness by sharing His character with us?

My experience has been that God moves toward us in hard times. Difficulties should make us think, *God is close!* When we spend time with Him in the crucible of discipline, He accomplishes His plans for us.

God moves toward us in hard times.

How has God trained you in holiness through past hardship?

What is He teaching you about holiness through your present trial?

Pray, asking God to make you holy through this experience.

TAKING STOCK, TAKING ACTION

Today's Scripture Focus

"For the moment all discipline seems painful rather than pleasant, but later it yields the peaceful fruit of righteousness to those who have been trained by it."

Hebrews 12:11

The writer of Hebrews knew Jesus was the best example of everything for us. When it comes to living as a child of God, Jesus demonstrated over and over that we can't go wrong if we follow and imitate Him. The problem is that trials often give me a case of nearsightedness. I can see only what is right in front of me, and then I miss what is coming later. But verse 2 admonishes us always to follow Jesus' example: "... looking to Jesus, the founder and perfecter of our faith, who for the joy that was set before him endured the cross, despising the shame, and is seated at the right hand of the throne of God."

Amazingly, Jesus could see beyond the cross. He endured the immediate, undeserved hardship and suffering because He knew the ultimate objective. Nevertheless, He still had to go through the cross, the trial God placed before Him. That's how Jesus learned obedience: "Although he was a son, he learned obedience through what he suffered" (Heb. 5:8). Jesus was always an obedient Son, and living here on earth gave Him abundant opportunities to demonstrate His obedience. By looking to Jesus, we can also become obedient sons and daughters as we experience hardship.

In what ways can a person practice "looking to Jesus" in life's trials?

How will Jesus' example affect the way you approach your hard situation?

Jesus still had to go through the cross, the trial God placed before Him.

Painful Discipline

Today's Scripture focus reminds us that "all discipline seems painful rather than pleasant" (Heb. 12:11). The trial you face may have made you all too aware of the pain of God's discipline. Haven't you found that it's easier to say to God, "Lord, I trust You, and I will obey You" when you are in calm waters? When everything seems to be going our way, it's easy to claim faith. But trusting God or obeying Him takes on a different flavor in the raging furnace of hardship or doubt. Think of Daniel's three friends. Daniel describes the good life for Shadrach, Meshach, and Abednego as overseers for the king. They had it made! Then the king got the idea to create a huge image of himself and demand that everyone bow before it or face the painful consequence of a fiery furnace. The three friends chose not to bow and were ushered toward the flames. Although they had done nothing wrong, it looked as if they would be toast if they didn't compromise and worship the statue.

The three young men made several points in what everybody thought would be their final words. They answered the king respectfully, consistent with their commitment to serve him. They simply couldn't worship him or his statue. They declared their trust was in God, who could save them from the furnace. They graciously informed the king their ultimate allegiance was to Someone greater than he, which didn't please the king at all. And they added this crucial footnote in the event God did not choose to save them: "If not, be it known to you, O king, that we will not serve your gods or worship the golden image that you have set up" (Dan. 3:18). He might be the king, but the three men in front of him were determined to worship the one true God.

So what happened after their bold testimony and courage? God let the king throw them into the furnace! The guys who tossed them into the oven were killed by the heat. Yet the three friends stayed cool in the flames. Hearing the crackling flames and watching their executioners die probably "seemed painful rather than pleasant" (Heb. 12:11), but they understood that God's purposes were much higher than providing them with an easy, safe life.

Identify a painful trial that has required you to learn obedience to God.

> When everything seems to be going our way, it's easy to claim faith.

How was your relationship with God affected during and as a result of that trial? Were you able to look to Jesus? Did you learn obedience?

The Peaceful Fruit of Righteousness

Hebrews 12:11 gives us a helpful way of thinking about the specific results of God's work in and around us to train us in holiness. Although the discipline seems painful, its seed "yields the peaceful fruit of righteousness [another way to describe holiness] to those who have been trained by it" (v. 11). Here are three crucial factors to keep in mind.

1. The pain of trials is momentary ("for the moment").

   What have been some momentary trials in your life that could serve as reminders that trials have ending points?

2. The profit from trials is immense ("the peaceful fruit of righteousness").

   What are some benefits that have come into your life as a result of past trials?

Our responses to trials have a lot to do with the benefit we receive from them.

3. The promise regarding trials is conditional ("to those who have been trained by it"). Our responses to trials have a lot to do with the benefit we receive from them.

Think about a trial in your life right now that you hope to be trained by. You may not yet know the timetable or how the profits will manifest themselves, but take a moment to tell God you are ready to be trained by this seed of difficulty in your life.

As you end this first week of assignments, let me assure you that God knows what you are going through. He knows you intimately, and He knows in exact detail what's going on. He grasps even the parts of your difficulties that are eluding you, and He knows the result He desires for you. As you walk through this difficult experience, you can learn from the inside out to say with Job:

> "He knows the way that I take; when he has tried me,
> I shall come out as gold." *Job 23:10*

What is happening in your life right now is not the result of God's inattentiveness or lack of concern for you. For this moment focus on that thought: God knows the way your life is going. And no matter how dark and overwhelming the pathway may seem now, He has good things ahead. He is gradually bringing you to a place of holiness, and that's more valuable than gold.

I. Nigel Rees, *Brewer's Famous Quotations* (London: Weidenfeld & Nicolson, 2006), 309.
2. A. W. Tozer, *The Knowledge of the Holy* (New York: Harper & Brothers, 1961), 111.

God knows what you are going through.

WHY TRIALS?

This Week's Scripture Focus

"Count it all joy, my brothers, when you meet trials of various kinds, for you know that the testing of your faith produces steadfastness. And let steadfastness have its full effect, that you may be perfect and complete, lacking in nothing.

"If any of you lacks wisdom, let him ask God, who gives generously to all without reproach, and it will be given him. But let him ask in faith, with no doubting, for the one who doubts is like a wave of the sea that is driven and tossed by the wind. For that person must not suppose that he will receive anything from the Lord; he is a double-minded man, unstable in all his ways." *James 1:2-8*

Submitting to the Father's Will

When we think about the fact that Jesus became a human being like us, His willingness to ask the question "Why?" just as we do may not be the first thing that comes to mind. We wonder why all the time. But did Jesus? We have the stunning example of His cry from the cross: "My God, my God, why have you forsaken me?" (Matt. 27:46). And when Jesus asked, "Why?" did God answer Him?

When we walk the streets of Jerusalem and stand on the ancient cobbled stones of the Fortress Antonia, it isn't hard to imagine that Jesus was here. The walls and floors take us back to Jesus' seeming helplessness and hopelessness as He was shuffled through a system determined to do away with Him. Neither His innocence nor His divinity was on the agenda of the people who collaborated in His death. Jesus had already agonized in the garden of Gethsemane and accepted the cup His Father had willed for Him. Then came Judas's betrayal, the rude arrest, and the disciples' abandonment. The physical and emotional weight of the moment must have been crushing as He endured the agony of those days before His death. His Father's plan was becoming a painful reality in the blows, the spitting, the curses, the ridicule, and the demands for His crucifixion that assaulted Jesus' body and filled His ears.

Then came the Via Dolorosa (the painful way) that Jesus had to walk to the cross. Today those reconstructed streets still echo as they must have that day, filled with crowds who assumed Jesus was simply one of three criminals on their way to execution or who wondered why someone with such an amazing reputation had met such a terrible fate. After those agonies came the nails and the lifting of the crossbars. Jesus was aware of His Father's will. He forgave His immediate tormentors. But at some point in the hours that followed, He would cry, "Why, Lord? Why?"

Week 2
GROUP EXPERIENCE

As You Gather

1. **What is one new thought about trials that you have had since you began this study?**

2. **Describe what you think it takes to have happiness in life.**

Preparation and Review

1. **What are hard experiences in your past that you now realize were trials?**

2. **How has your relationship with God been affected by last week's group session and your study of the daily assignments in week 1?**

3. **What questions or issues about trials do you hope will be resolved or clarified as we continue in this study?**

DVD Session 2 Viewer Guide

I. Consider your trials _____ (see Jas. 1:2).

You do not have it in _____ to be joyful.

Joy is a supernatural delight in the _____, _____, and _____ of God.

For a Christian, life is about displaying the _____ of a life lived in God.

Four checkup questions:
1. What happened to _____?
2. Why am I here on _____?
3. How can this trial advance that life _____?
4. What can I do at this moment to _____ the superiority of a life lived in God?

II. Your trials produce _____ power (see Jas. 1:3).

Three questions on faith's final exam:

1. Do you believe God is in _____?

2. Do you believe God is _____?

3. Will you wait on God _____ _____ until the darkness becomes light?

The original word translated *steadfastness, endurance, perseverance,* and *patience* literally means *to* _____ *under.*

Four alternatives we can choose instead of demonstrating steadfastness:

1. We _____ against God.

2. We _____ _____ at others.

3. We _____, declaring, "I didn't sign up for this!"

4. We _____, collapsing without benefiting from the trial.

III. Trials produce life _____ (see Jas. 1:5-6).

When it comes to wisdom:

• Ask _____.

• Make sure you really want to _____ without conditions.

• When pursuing wisdom, beware of double-_____.

Responding to the DVD Teaching

1. How would you explain the following declaration? Perseverance is the funnel through which all Christian virtue flows. What are some examples?

2. You were challenged to create four review cards that can help you clarify steps to take when facing a hard time. How can these questions help you understand God's purpose for your trial?

• What happened to me?

• Why am I here on earth?

• How can this trial advance that life purpose?

• What can I do at this moment to display the superiority of a life lived in God?

3. What comfort and challenge does Psalm 27:13 offer for your trial?

"I believe that I shall look upon the goodness of the LORD
 in the land of the living!"

Read week 2 and complete the activities before the next group experience.

If you missed this session, you can download the DVD teaching from
www.lifeway.com/downloads.

Day 1

CONSIDER YOUR TRIALS ... WHAT?

Today's Scripture Focus

"Count it all joy, my brothers, when you meet trials of various kinds."

James 1:2

If you don't think this is one of the most outrageous statements in the New Testament, you didn't read it carefully enough! We are not used to reading the words *joy* and *trial* in the same sentence. As we sail through life, trials look to us like nasty storms. They threaten to sink our ship. Sometimes we think we've got to lighten the load to survive, and the first thing we throw overboard is joy. We can't imagine that we can have troubles and be joyful at the same time. James obviously thought otherwise!

What Is Joy?

Joy is something very different from what we commonly refer to as happiness. So when Scripture says, "Count it all joy," it isn't saying, "Be happy about your trials." Happiness is circumstantial. It's an in-the-moment, "Oh, I'm so excited" feeling based on something that happens in your life. In fact, happiness is all about feelings, and that's why it comes and goes so easily. We can pursue happiness, but we can't retain it permanently even when we find it. Happiness is a by-product when a lot of other things turn out just right.

> **Joy is a supernatural delight in the person, purposes, and people of God.**

When it comes to joy, we're aiming at something deep and lasting. A biblical definition of *joy* is a supernatural delight in the person, purposes, and people of God. Unlike happiness, joy isn't based on circumstances; James 1:2 implies that we choose to count it all joy. When we find out why God uses trials in our lives, we've got good reason to choose joy, even though we may not be happy about the circumstances. So let's get clear in our minds what this verse means by "joy" and "trials of various kinds."

Joy is a supernatural delight in the person, purposes, and people of God. What is the central focus of joy in this definition?

Complete each of the following sentences.

Delighting in the person of God means ...

Delighting in the purposes of God means ...

Delighting in the people of God means ...

How did the following Bible characters demonstrate joy during difficult times?

Abraham (see Gen. 22:1-19):

Joseph, son of Jacob (see Gen. 40:1-23):

Esther (see Esth. 4:1-17):

Mary (see Luke 1:26-38):

Zechariah (see Luke 1:57-80):

Paul (see Acts 16:16-34):

Jesus (see Heb. 12:1-2):

Where Does Joy Come From?

The choice to "count it all joy" (Jas. 1:2) is not simply rooted in your will. You don't have it in yourself to be joyful. You don't just decide to be joyful in a vacuum. You must have a reason for joy that is greater than whatever else you might be facing. Your choice to "count it all joy" depends on your view of God and your relationship with Him. You see, joy is all about God.

You don't have it in yourself to be joyful.

People often try to find joy in things other than God—people, philosophies, causes, possessions, and power, to name a few. Why are these inadequate foundations for joy?

Can you think of a hard time in your life when you experienced supernatural delight in the person, purposes, and people of God in spite of your circumstances? Describe how God gave you this joy.

Galatians 5:22 lists joy as second among the fruit of the Spirit. Joy is supernatural.

Based on our definition of *joy*, name some ways joy can be a fruit or product in your life.

What clues would indicate that a person was counting it all joy in the middle of trials? How can you spot supernatural delight?

The Christian life is about displaying the superiority of a life lived in God.

The Christian life is about displaying the superiority of a life lived in God. When we talk about the blessings and benefits of being followers of Jesus, we often focus on what may appear to outsiders a misplaced confidence that nothing bad, hard, or hurtful will happen to us. This is true in the ultimate sense—our eternal destiny is safe in God's hands—but not in the immediate sense. Hard things definitely happen to faithful people. The superiority of a life lived in God isn't superior because it's pain-free or easy; it's superior because it approaches the hard parts of life with joy! Joyless Christians do a lousy job of pointing others to Christ. Both Christians and non-Christians get cancer. But there should be a distinct difference between the ways Christians and non-Christians respond to life-threatening news.

What differences have you noticed between the ways Christians and non-Christians face hard times?

What happens if Christians fail to count it all joy when they face trials?

When Jesus said, "I came that they may have life and have it abundantly" (John 10:10), He was saying what His half-brother James meant by "count it all joy." Jesus, however, was declaring Himself to be the source of that joy, that abundant life. Our capacity to live to the fullest even in the middle of hardship is always connected to the vitality of our relationship with Jesus.

> Our capacity to live to the fullest even in the middle of hardship is always connected to the vitality of our relationship with Jesus.

Think about a trial you are experiencing. Have you invited Jesus to participate with you in this hard time? ☐ **Yes** ☐ **No**

If so, what have been the results?

If not, ask Him to help you face your trial with joy as you delight in Him. How does this particular hardship bring you opportunities to delight—

in God's person?

in God's purposes?

in God's people?

Day 2
TESTED FAITH

Today's Scripture Focus

"You know that the testing of your faith produces steadfastness."

James 1:3

In yesterday's Scripture focus we were admonished to count it all joy when we meet "trials of various kinds" (Jas. 1:2). In the Septuagint, the Greek translation of the Old Testament, "various kinds" is the same phrase that is used to describe Joseph's coat of many colors. Hardship comes in many shades. Some trials are tough, and some are tragic. Some are difficult, and some are devastating.

Our trials are also very different. My trials are different from yours. Watch out for the temptation to think, *I wish I had her trial! Compared to mine, that would be a piece of cake!* It's never helpful to compare God's work in others to what He is doing in and around you. To do so is to question God's wisdom in the trials He allows into our lives. Don't get between the hammer and the work on that one. Just leave other people's situations with God and focus on what He is doing in you.

The Test

James progresses from trials in verse 2 to testing in verse 3: "You know that the testing of your faith produces steadfastness." If you don't know it now, you will know it tomorrow. Trials separate the men from the boys. Trials separate the sheep from the goats. Trials separate the wheat from the tares. The proof of whether you are a true follower of Christ often comes with trials, for trials test our faith like nothing else.

> **The proof of whether you are a true follower of Christ often comes with trials.**

How did you feel to face a test in school when you had adequately prepared?

☐ **Afraid**   ☐ **Confident**   ☐ **Insecure**

God is a teacher like no other. He doesn't need to test us to see what we're made of or what we know. We don't have to prove anything to Him; He already knows everything about us! So why is the testing necessary? For our own good. Remember our definition of *trial* from last week? A trial is a painful circumstance allowed by God to change our conduct and our character. God doesn't allow tests to cause us to fail but to give us the opportunity to succeed with His help.

God tested Abraham by asking him to release his son Isaac to God (see Gen. 22:1-19). Now that was quite a test. Abraham had been waiting for decades to receive the promised son. Then, before that son had become a man, God was asking for him back. It's easy to make promises to God if we don't really think He will take us up on them. We can say, "Lord, all I have is Yours"; but what happens when He answers, "OK, I'll take it?" When the precious child God gave us is sick or the lovely home goes up in flames, can we say with Job, "The LORD gave, and the LORD has taken away" (Job 1:22)? Or do we mutter, "When I gave it to You, Lord, I didn't really expect You to take me up on the offer"?

What are some parts of your life that you have declared are God's but would be difficult for you to let go?

Read Proverbs 3:5-6:

> "Trust in the LORD with all your heart,
> and do not lean on your own understanding.
> In all your ways acknowledge him,
> and he will make straight your paths."

In what ways are you actively exercising trust in God regarding the people and possessions in your life?

When Tests Come

The tests that come into our lives may surprise us by their timing, but we should never be surprised when the tests come. We can be prepared. If we will settle the answers to three key questions in our hearts and minds, we will be able to respond with confidence to testing.

1. Do you believe that God is in control?
2. Do you believe that God is good?
3. Will you wait on God by faith until the darkness becomes light?

When trials come, why is it important to affirm that God is in control?

When life turns difficult, why is it crucial to remember that God is good?

Why are we tempted not to wait on God until the darkness becomes light?

Only when your faith is strong are you willing to wait for God to work out His good purposes through your trial.

Notice that James didn't say it's your nerve, your courage, or your strength that's being tested. We're talking about faith here. God brings tests into your life because your faith in Him—your belief that He is in control and that He is good—can be proved only in times when life is hard. Only when your faith is strong are you willing to wait for God to work out His good purposes through your trial.

King David did a lot of waiting. Years went by after Samuel called him in from watching the sheep and anointed him as king. Several times King Saul almost killed him, so David lived on the run. But David was more than a survivor; he was an overcomer. He was confident that God's plan would unfold in due time. Even when he had the opportunity to take matters into his own hands and kill his pursuer, he refused. Saul was still God's chosen king, and David wasn't about to remove him from the throne. That would be God's doing. David exercised faith and waited on God:

> "I believe that I shall look upon the goodness of the LORD
> in the land of the living!" *Psalm 27:13*

Having stated his own decision to trust God, David concluded by writing to us in Psalm 27:14:

> "Wait for the LORD;
> be strong, and let your heart take courage;
> wait for the LORD."

David understood the principle of James 1:3 centuries before the words were written: "You know that the testing of your faith produces steadfastness."

Describe a time when your faith was tested through a trial.

Apply the three questions on page 43 to the trial you described. How did you respond to this testing?

How did this test strengthen your faith and prepare you for further testing?

In what ways is your faith being tested right now?

Spend some time waiting on God. Thank Him for testing your faith. Ask Him to strengthen your faith and to teach you perseverance through your trial. Listen and give Him an opportunity to speak to you in the silence.

Day 3

REMAIN UNDER

Today's Scripture Focus

"You know that the testing of your faith produces steadfastness.
And let steadfastness have its full effect, that you may
be perfect and complete, lacking in nothing."

James 1:3-4

Today we want to spend most of our time thinking about the meaning of the word in James 1:3 that the English Standard Version translates "steadfastness." Other translations use terms like "patience" (KJV, NKJV), "endurance" (HCSB), and "forced into the open and shows its true colors" (Message). Although *steadfastness* is not a word we use in common speech, it is nevertheless an almost literal translation of the original. The Greek term here is a compound word meaning *remain under,* as in *staying in place when the pressure is on* or *standing fast,* from which we get the noun form *steadfastness.* The *fast* part of this word is interesting because it highlights the classic meaning of *fast,* which is not primarily *quick* but *rootedness, immovability, firmness,* and even *loyalty.* A modern expression that comes close is *hanging tough.* James is telling us that the immediate result of the testing of our faith is an increased capacity for standing our ground when the pressure is on. This capacity cannot be fully developed unless pressure is applied. When the test pressure is on, most of us quickly realize how far we still have to grow.

> **When the test pressure is on, most of us quickly realize how far we still have to grow.**

The principle James used here can be seen in many parts of life. Did you have a teacher growing up who cheerfully made life miserable for you? Did he or she demand more from you than you really wanted to give? Did that instructor dare to demand excellence from you when you were ready to settle for mediocrity? If you won that contest of wills, you didn't do yourself a favor. That teacher was giving you a gift of pressure to help you grow.

Describe a time when you remained under a difficult situation or person and benefited from the test.

Under Pressure

Remaining under and developing steadfastness doesn't come easily to us. Our instinct is to avoid the pressure. If we focus only on the pressure and never consider that God may have a good purpose in allowing it, we will tend to apply one or a combination of four strategies to get out from under it.

Complain. In my book *Lord, Change My Attitude* I defined *complaining:* "to express dissatisfaction with a circumstance which is not wrong and about which I'm not doing anything to correct."[1]

How does complaining try to avoid the necessity of remaining under pressure until it produces steadfastness?

Lash out or blame others. Other people's choices and decisions may in fact bring a lot of pressure into our lives, but blaming them does not really address what God might have in mind by allowing them to put us in that position. And lashing out at others just because we're angry or anxious is simply a sign that we're failing the test.

How does lashing out actually compound the pressure rather than relieve it?

Bail. Certain streams of thought always seem to surface when we're under pressure: "Lord, this is not what I signed up for! When You said in John 16:33, 'In the world you will have tribulation,' this can't be what You meant, can it? I can't see anything good coming out of this situation, so I'm leaving the premises. I'm running as far and as fast as I can from this pressure. I'm going to turn my denial dial all the way up and ignore anything You try to say to me!" If we act on these streams of thought, we'll find ourselves up a creek without a paddle.

Identify a situation when you were under pressure and bailed out, thereby failing to benefit from the test.

Fold. Folding is bailing on everything. You start with the circumstance you don't want to be in and enlarge your reaction so that it covers most of life: "God, I not only reject this lousy situation you've placed me in, but I also reject You.

> Developing steadfastness doesn't come easily to us.

I thought You were in control and were good; but based on what I'm having to deal with here, You can't be either. So I'm cashing in my faith chips and going my own way. I may not believe in You anymore. Or I may keep believing You exist but only so that I can stay angry at You!" Folding does little about the pressure, and it actually cuts us off from the one Source who can help us remain steadfast under the hard times.

How often is folding your active or passive strategy for handling difficulties instead of remaining under?

☐ **Never** ☐ **Sometimes** ☐ **Frequently** ☐ **Always**

Identify whether the following people in the Bible complained, lashed out, bailed, folded, or remained steadfast.

Joseph (see Gen. 50:15-21):

Balaam (see Num. 22:22-35):

Elijah (see 1 Kings 19:8):

Peter (see Matt. 26:69-75):

Judas (see Matt. 27:1-5):

Israel (see 1 Cor. 10:6-10):

Moses (see Heb. 11:24-28):

As you think about a trial you are going through, ask God to help you identify one way He wants you to practice steadfastness. Ask Him for His help and His strength.

Perfect and Complete

The prospect of developing steadfastness is daunting. Many of us have failed so miserably in the past that we cringe at the thought of another failure. But God knows our condition and our history. We don't have to puff ourselves up and respond with bravado in the face of hard times. We can remember the words of Peter, who had his own track record in the area of less-than-steadfastness: "Clothe yourselves, all of you, with humility toward one another, for 'God opposes the proud but gives grace to the humble.' Humble yourselves, therefore, under the mighty hand of God so that at the proper time he may exalt you" (1 Pet. 5:5-6). Peter knew that genuine humility cuts two ways—toward others and under God's mighty hand.

We don't have to puff ourselves up and respond with bravado in the face of hard times.

Sometimes when you are suffering, it's hard not to think that you're the center of the universe or that you are hurting worse than anyone else. Humility demands that you remain concerned about others. List several persons you know who are facing hardship. Let your own discomfort fire up your prayers for them.

How does remaining under the pressure of a trial allow a believer to become humble before God?

Humility is a sorely lacking quality among those who complain, lash out, bail, or fold under pressure. Humility is a core virtue of mature Christians who have stayed under the funnel of adversity long enough to benefit from it. I am convinced that perseverance is the narrow channel through which all other Christian virtues flow. Both Peter and James are telling us that our desire to avoid pain and escape pressure can't have the deciding vote in our lives. If, instead, we remain under God's wise and good purposes for us, He will direct us toward becoming "perfect and complete, lacking in nothing" (Jas. 1:4). This phrase doesn't mean brittle, shallow, do-it-yourself perfectionism; it's about robust maturity, a combination of deep qualities that mark someone who has seen and experienced what life can dish out and is still standing under God's mighty hand. The picture of standing under God's mighty hand is sobering because it acknowledges the fact that God allows pain and pressure in our lives. But that is also a place of protection and our ultimate source of strength for steadfastness.

> Perseverance is the narrow channel through which all other Christian virtues flow.

Write an expression of your desire not to escape the pressure but to trust God and "let steadfastness have its full effect" through a hard circumstance in your life.

Use your statement to pray in a manner that says, "Lord, use this trial to accomplish the best possible results in my life. Give it all to me; pour it on; do Your work."

Day 4

WISDOM FIRST AID

Today's Scripture Focus

"If any of you lacks wisdom, let him ask God, who gives generously
to all without reproach, and it will be given him. But let him ask
in faith, with no doubting, for the one who doubts is like a wave
of the sea that is driven and tossed by the wind."

James 1:5-6

By this point you may be feeling overwhelmed. I mean, it's one thing to think about remaining under a difficult situation; it's something else entirely to actually remain under it! Maybe you're thinking, *Endurance? Sounds like a good idea. Is there an easy way to get it? Is there a fast way to steadfastness? Show me the shortcut to patience and the fun road to long-suffering!* Sorry, there's no quick or painless process for spiritual growth. God doesn't offer instant sanctification. We can wish all we want for a sprint to maturity; but eventually, we have to accept that God designed life as a marathon and that every step is worth running.

Even when we understand in principle why God would let us go through trials, we still wonder how we are going to make it. We can predict that as the pressure increases, the intensity of the *why* questions will also increase. For those questions we need to consider one of the most widely misused passages in Scripture: "If any of you lacks wisdom, let him ask God" (Jas. 1:5).

I used to frequently invoke this passage back in my school days, thinking it was the ideal antidote for inadequate preparation and slack study habits. *Forget about the drudgery of review and flashcards,* I thought. *Skip the repetition and memorization. Simply ask God to fill all the blanks!* It never worked! And it wasn't for a lack of trying this approach on my part. The lack James is talking about is a humble realization that at our very best, the situation we're in is going to take more to endure than we have in ourselves.

At our very best, the situation we're in is going to take more to endure than we have in ourselves.

During hardship what signs tell us we're short on wisdom?

When you find yourself under pressure or in a hard time, what kind of wisdom do you lack?

The Cry for Wisdom

Wisdom, as the Bible uses the term, refers to practical rather than theoretical knowledge. In a sense, the Book of James functions in the New Testament the way the Book of Proverbs functions in the Old Testament. Based on the beliefs that God is in control and that God is good, both books address questions that come up when people face the real issues of life. So James offers a perspective on the kind of *why* questions that God will and will not answer when we face hard times. Looking at some of those questions will help us understand what kind of wisdom God provides when we hurt.

The existential why. God doesn't answer the existential why: "Why do bad things happen to good people?" I think there are some good answers to that question, but that's not what James was teaching us about. When we are under pressure, we need a practical, wise answer for our circumstance, not an answer that fits every situation.

The ultimatum why. God never promises to give us answers to ultimatum-why questions this side of eternity. People who withhold faith in God because He hasn't answered all of their *why* questions must learn to live with disappointment. God doesn't negotiate with those who refuse to recognize who is in charge of the universe. And just because we know who God is, He still doesn't owe us answers we couldn't understand anyway. This realization is the stunning conclusion of Job's saga. God doesn't have to tell us anything. What is amazing is that He chooses to tell us so much!

The observation why. God rarely answers observation-why questions, such as "Why doesn't my hard-to-get-along-with neighbor have to go through this trial, God?" Or "Lord, why did You allow that natural disaster to occur in that place?"

The personal why. The *why* that God will answer is the personal why: "Why did You allow this in my life now, God? What do You want to teach me?" You get to Him with that kind of question. "If I remain under here, God, what are the things You want to work on? What's next in Your plan of transformation for me?" God answers that *why* in a hurry.

> The *why* that God will answer is the personal why.

God isn't playing poker. He wants you to see His cards. He will flood your life with wisdom when you ask for the kind of information He wants to give you. "Why am I like this, God, and why has it been so hard for me to change? Why have I not been able to see this and have been so stubborn when others have pointed it out to me? Why have I been so slow to realize the price I have paid and how this flaw in me has injured others?" These are the *whys* of trials that God longs to answer.

These are the cries God generously answers, supplying the wisdom we need to grow through our trial.

What are some _whys_ you have for God as you deal with your particular trial?

Carefully look at your list and discard any questions that you shouldn't expect God to answer. What kind of wisdom has God supplied during your trial, even through this study?

No Reproach

Today's Scripture focus says God will answer your personal prayer for wisdom "without reproach" (v. 5), which means that He won't sink His teeth into you for asking. He will answer you generously. If you come before God with "What are You trying to teach me now, God?" He's not going to respond, "You again? Don't you know how many things I have to do up here? Do you know how far down the list you are in order of importance? Quit bothering me with your little questions about your trials." God isn't like that. He loves you. He knows you're going through a hard time. He knows you need Him because you can't do it alone. One of the greatest moments between you and the Lord is when you come to a point of submission and He takes you into His arms, soothes your soul, binds your wounds, and fills your mind with wisdom for what's ahead. If you can say, "Here I am, God. I'm not going anywhere, but I don't want to have to learn this again. Help me learn this right now. What are we going for here?" Ask God that, and He will answer you generously without reproach.

Since you know God will not reproach you for asking, in what areas of your life would you like to ask Him for wisdom as you wait for the darkness to become light?

> The issue is whether we are willing to trust God to deliver what we need when we need it.

Spend time in prayer seeking wisdom for your difficult circumstance.

The real issue is never whether we have enough wisdom to face a dark time—we don't. The issue is whether we are willing to trust God to deliver what we need when we need it. And the proof is in the way we wait for His wisdom.

Day 5

HOW BADLY DO YOU WANT TO KNOW?

Today's Scripture Focus

"Let him ask in faith, with no doubting, for the one who doubts
is like a wave of the sea that is driven and tossed by the wind.
For that person must not suppose that he will receive anything from
the Lord; he is a double-minded man, unstable in all his ways."

James 1:6-8

When we ask God for wisdom about why our trial has come, James says to ask "in faith, with no doubting, for the one who doubts is like a wave of the sea that is driven and tossed by the wind." Ever watch a beach ball in the crowd at a sports arena? It floats here, then gets batted over there, then drifts up or down. Now it's over there. A lot of us are like that in the middle of a trial. We sort of want to know what God wants to teach us, but we've got these creeping doubts: "OK, God, I'm ready to hear what it is. But before You start, could I read off the things it can't be? You can't ask me to keep loving my daughter." Or "You can't ask me to put up with my boss at work." Or "I'm just not willing to face up to my materialism and lack of compassion for the poor. I just can't do it!" Up and down, tossed by the wind and waves. Nothing's coming to that doubter.

No Doubting

James urges us not to doubt when we ask for wisdom. The kind of doubting James is talking about is not so much the capacity to wonder or fear but the tendency to harbor areas of our lives where we don't believe God can work. Our reservations reveal that we don't really believe God knows best. If we go to God for help but insist on retaining control and having the last word, we shouldn't expect Him to answer.

> If we go to God for help but insist on retaining control and having the last word, we shouldn't expect Him to answer.

If you think you are staying in control this way, you are mistaken. You've got no more control over where your life's going than the beach ball in the crowd. Someone says something to you, and you are encouraged; and then—oh, no— you hear someone else's words, and now you're discouraged. Now you're on; now you're off. You love God, but you're also bitter. That's how you're living if you're not in true submission to God in the midst of your trial. The only way you will ever learn from His discipline is to humble yourself and say, "God, whatever You want to teach me—nothing is off limits. Take it all! Anything, God. I don't want to have to come back this way again." Only when you pray for wisdom with no strings attached, no limits of any kind on what God can do, can you expect to get the wisdom you need for your trial.

As you have asked God to teach you through your trial, what conditions have you placed on your request? For example, maybe you aren't willing to change the way you relate to others, although that is one thing He wants to teach you.

Now instead of expecting God to accept your conditions, start praying that He will give you wisdom to deal with these areas of your life.

Down with Double-Mindedness

James 1:8 tells us a doubter is "a double-minded man, unstable in all his ways." Someone who doubts God's good purposes is like a two-souled person: "I want what God wants, but I don't want what God wants. I want to learn from my situation, but I'm angry with . . . !" The focus is less on what God is teaching and more on hurt feelings. When your focus is on taking revenge, or making your point, or getting the pressure off, you are very unstable—not only incapable of learning from your trial but also dysfunctional in relating to God and others.

The wisdom we desperately need from God is wasted if we refuse to align with His direction. Keeping our options open cuts us off from godly wisdom. God wants us to choose Him and His ways every time. Only a single-minded devotion to Him puts us in a position to learn from Him when we face hardship.

What would you say is the default setting of your thought processes?
☐ **Single-mindedness** ☐ **Double-mindedness**

Think about the way you have faced a current or past trial. Check any of the following ways your responses have reflected single-mindedness toward God during this time.

The wisdom we desperately need from God is wasted if we refuse to align with His direction.

- ☐ **I sought His wisdom without doubting.**

- ☐ **I aligned my will with His.**

- ☐ **I made single-minded commitments based on Scripture.**

- ☐ **I refused to choose the world's approach to my problem.**

- ☐ **Other:**

The cure for double-mindedness isn't just single-mindedness; it's God-mindedness. It's getting your thinking in line with God's thinking. Right thinking is having a mind that is captive to God's Word. When you ask for wisdom for your trial, you are asking God to align your thinking with His will and His Word.

I've been taking it for granted that you are facing hard times in your life right now. If you are a child of God, you are experiencing hardship in some area of your life. This study may even be adding pressure if it is making you realize that you have been responding to trials in the wrong way. I challenge you to get serious about what God wants to do in your life and to seek His wisdom for the way He wants you to handle your trials. The apostle Paul wrote, "The Spirit himself bears witness with our spirit that we are children of God" (Rom. 8:16). We are meant to hear the whispers of our Heavenly Father during times when life is hard. He is certainly drawing near to us in those moments.

Think back over the past two weeks. Describe moments of intimacy with God since you have been engaged in this study. When have you sensed God saying, "This is happening to you because you are My child"?

The cure for double-mindedness isn't just single-mindedness; it's God-mindedness.

1. James MacDonald, *Lord, Change My Attitude* (Nashville: LifeWay Press, 2008), 9.

Week 3

WHAT TO DO WITH TRIALS

This Week's Scripture Focus

"Since therefore Christ suffered in the flesh, arm yourselves with the same way of thinking, for whoever has suffered in the flesh has ceased from sin, so as to live for the rest of the time in the flesh no longer for human passions but for the will of God. For the time that is past suffices for doing what the Gentiles want to do, living in sensuality, passions, drunkenness, orgies, drinking parties, and lawless idolatry. With respect to this they are surprised when you do not join them in the same flood of debauchery, and they malign you; but they will give account to him who is ready to judge the living and the dead. For this is why the gospel was preached even to those who are dead, that though judged in the flesh the way people are, they might live in the spirit the way God does. The end of all things is at hand; therefore be self-controlled and sober-minded for the sake of your prayers. Above all, keep loving one another earnestly, since love covers a multitude of sins. Show hospitality to one another without grumbling. As each has received a gift, use it to serve one another, as good stewards of God's varied grace: whoever speaks, as one who speaks oracles of God; whoever serves, as one who serves by the strength that God supplies—in order that in everything God may be glorified through Jesus Christ. To him belong glory and dominion forever and ever. Amen. Beloved, do not be surprised at the fiery trial when it comes upon you to test you, as though something strange were happening to you. But rejoice insofar as you share Christ's sufferings, that you may also rejoice and be glad when his glory is revealed. If you are insulted for the name of Christ, you are blessed, because the Spirit of glory and of God rests upon you. But let none of you suffer as a murderer or a thief or an evildoer or as a meddler. Yet if anyone suffers as a Christian, let him not be ashamed, but let him glorify God in that name. For it is time for judgment to begin at the household of God; and if it begins with us, what will be the outcome for those who do not obey the gospel of God? And 'If the righteous is scarcely saved, what will become of the ungodly and the sinner?' Therefore let those who suffer according to God's will entrust their souls to a faithful Creator while doing good." *1 Peter 4:1-19*

Standing Alone

I hope you have a chance to visit the Holy Land sometime in your life. No, I don't think going where Jesus walked is a requirement for a Christian; we are required to walk as He walked wherever we are. But visiting Jerusalem and other places where Jesus spent time provides background for us and gives us a sense of proportion about the way we imagine events in Scripture. Seeing what He saw often helps us better understand what He said.

After a couple of turbulent millennia, lots of things have changed in Israel. Some biblical locations are tentative; for example, there are several garden tombs and more than one possible Golgotha. Others are clearly wild guesses; Jesus could have been alone in the wilderness in any number of desolate spots. But there are still some places where you know you are walking where Jesus walked. Caiaphas's house has been excavated and identified. Nearby an ancient stone stairwell marks the passageway where we can be certain Jesus was brought on the way to His sham trial. He was alone. Peter and John were following from a distance, but Peter would shortly deny he even knew Jesus. Surrounded by human and demonic authorities, Jesus stood alone.

Trials separate us from others. We feel alone, singled out, cut off, and abandoned. But, as the Scripture we will study this week reminds us, those can be times of special intimacy with Jesus, for He knows firsthand what we are going through. He has already passed this way.

Week 3

GROUP EXPERIENCE

As You Gather

1. Would you call yourself a person who likes to be surprised or a person who likes to be prepared? Why? How do you think this preference affects your life?

2. Share illustrations of the value of being prepared for the unexpected.

Preparation and Review

1. Which lesson or Bible passage from week 2 had the biggest impact on you? In what way?

2. If someone asked you, "Why do trials come to people who closely follow the Lord?" how would you answer from James 1:2-8?

3. Name one practical insight from week 2's assignments that you are implementing in your life. What have been the results so far?

DVD Session 3 Viewer Guide

Suffering will ___*come*___ (see 1 Pet. 4:1-7).

The apostle Paul told Timothy, "___*all*___ who desire to live godly in Christ Jesus will suffer persecution" (2 Tim. 3:12, NKJV).

The number one tool in God's chest for chiseling our character is ___*suffering*___, so we can ___*Brace*___ ourselves.

___*guard*___ your behavior (see 1 Pet. 4:1-6).

Trials remind us that life is not going to go on ___*forever*___.

Sin over ___*promises*___ and under ___*delivers*___ every time.

grace your relationships (see 1 Pet. 4:7-11a).

Above all: love _earnestly_!

In trials you will never go wrong sharing _Scripture_ with people.

If you want to help someone in trials, make sure you are _right_ with God.

Glorify your God (see 1 Pet. 4:11b-19).

My existence should be a _shout_ about God's existence, in comparison to the muted voice of creation.

Rejoice when God's glory is revealed in your suffering even as it was revealed in Christ's suffering (see v. 13).

Don't be _ashamed_.

Self-_examine_.

entrust yourself to God.

Responding to the Video Teaching

1. What new insight did you gain from 1 Peter 4 that will help you respond to trials?

2. How do you find yourself responding to the repeated message that trials and hardships are and will be part of this life as long as we are on earth?

3. In what ways could the rest of the group pray for you as you face your trial?

Read week 3 and complete the activities before the next group experience.

If you missed this session, you can download the **DVD** teaching from *www.lifeway.com/downloads.*

Day 1

TRIALS ARE COMING

Today's Scripture Focus

"Since therefore Christ suffered in the flesh ..."

1 Peter 4:1

Whether or not you like surprises, one of the lasting lessons I trust you will take away from this study is never again to be surprised by suffering. Settle into the fact that trials are coming. You may be going through some now, but getting through them doesn't mean you won't have more. Hate to burst your hope bubble, and I'm not against hope, but our hope must be based on Christ's presence in our lives rather than on our current circumstances.

In 1 Peter 3:15 the apostle wrote, "In your hearts honor Christ the Lord as holy, always being prepared to make a defense to anyone who asks you for a reason for the hope that is in you; yet do it with gentleness and respect." Peter gave this instruction to people for whom he was writing an entire book about suffering (see 1 Pet. 1:6,10-11; 2:19-21,23; 3:14,17; 4:1,12-13,16,19; 5:10). Yet Peter emphasized that in the midst of suffering, real hope comes from firmly resting in and honoring Christ the Lord.

> Our hope must be based on Christ's presence in our lives rather than on our current circumstances.

Since Christ Suffered

Today's Scripture focus begins, "Since therefore ..." The word *since* is one of those tip-off words the Bible uses to get our attention. It indicates that something is about to be said that will affect what follows. *Therefore* is another of those words. Bible students are often told, "When you see a *therefore*, make sure you know what it's there for." The apostle is telling us, "Because of the facts before us, the rest of what I am about to tell you is worth your attention." The *since* and the *therefore* that Peter doesn't want us to miss is "Christ suffered in the flesh."

In week 1 we talked about the difference between suffering as a consequence and suffering as a trial or discipline. What is the difference between a consequence and a trial?

consequence — something you did — Trial — " you need to learn

Was Jesus' suffering on the cross a consequence or a trial? Why?

Jesus' suffering
was different from
anything we will
ever experience.

Jesus' suffering was different from anything we will ever experience. One of the simplest but most profound acknowledgments of the uniqueness of Jesus' suffering came from one of the two criminals who hung on a cross next to Jesus. This condemned man said to the other in Christ's presence, " 'Do you not fear God, since you are under the same sentence of condemnation? And we indeed justly, for we are receiving the due reward of our deeds; but this man has done nothing wrong.' And he said, 'Jesus, remember me when you come into your kingdom' " (Luke 23:40-42). This criminal understood the difference between suffering consequences (what put him and the other criminal on crosses) and suffering under discipline (which put Jesus on the cross). Jesus' trial on Calvary accomplished something for us that could not be accomplished any other way. He suffered the ultimate consequences for *our* sins! Jesus suffered for sinners who would be eternally separated from God. Jesus died for the thief on the cross— and for us.

What kind of suffering did Jesus prevent from ever coming to us by taking our place on the cross?

Separation from God

Jesus responded to the man's confession with an unforgettable promise: "Truly, I say to you, today you will be with me in Paradise" (Luke 23:43). That man not only knew and accepted the consequences for his own sins, but he also realized Jesus was uniquely capable of offering hope to others.

Brace Yourself

In a sense, the apostle Peter is asking us to join the believing thief on the cross in recognizing Jesus' uniqueness. But we must also recognize that if the holy and innocent Son of God suffered undeserved pain and trials, God may not withhold suffering from our lives as well.

Read 2 Timothy 3:12:

"All who desire to live a godly life in Christ Jesus will be persecuted."

Why do you think God expects His children to suffer?

The warning Paul gave Timothy in 2 Timothy 3:12 is flat-out love. Peter's reminder to us that Jesus suffered is also tough compassion. And here's the reason. If you're driving down the freeway and somebody cuts in front of you and you see a collision coming, you brace yourself. If you stumble down a step and start to fall, the first thing you do is put your hands out to break your fall. You brace yourself.

The reason God's Word repeats the fact that suffering is God's number one tool for chiseling our character is so that we can brace ourselves. God loves us, so He warns us.

God loves us,
so He warns us.

What are some stone chips in your life that you know God's suffering chisel has removed from your life?

Check your trial-alert status by identifying the statement that best describes your life right now.

☐ Still wondering what God is trying to prove by letting trials come into my life

☐ Desperately trying to keep my head in the sand and hoping nothing else bad happens

☐ Taking a deep breath after a hard time, quietly waiting for the next challenge

☑ Wondering whether I can take much more but conscious that God knows best

☑ Alert to what else God has to teach me during this particular time of difficulty in my life

☐ Other:

We have learned in previous weeks that God uses trials to discipline us for our benefit. Remember that a trial is a painful circumstance allowed by God to change our conduct and our character. Wise parents know they cannot prevent all pain in a child's life and shouldn't. Small pains often keep us from experiencing even deeper pains. Eternal lessons can be learned through suffering. Suffering has a clarifying, maturing role in our lives like no other kind of experience. Trials teach us how to rely on God and how to persevere in faith.

Welcome to the biblical gospel. We belong to God. Our lives are not our own; we have been bought with a price (see 1 Cor. 6:19-20). Jesus suffered, the apostles suffered, and great men and women throughout every era of history have been refined by their Maker in the furnace of adversity. Following Jesus means suffering is the norm, not the exception!

> **Following Jesus means suffering is the norm, not the exception!**

Jesus suffered even though He deserved none of what He had to endure. And He did it for you. One benefit of suffering is that it helps you identify with Jesus' suffering. How do you think hardship helps you identify with Jesus' suffering on earth?

Read 1 Peter 1:6-7:

> "In this you rejoice, though now for a little while, if necessary, you have been grieved by various trials, so that the tested genuineness of your faith—more precious than gold that perishes though it is tested by fire—may be found to result in praise and glory and honor at the revelation of Jesus Christ."

Would the refinement of your faith make suffering worth the pain? Talk to God about your response.

LIVE FOR THE WILL OF GOD

Today's Scripture Focus

"Since therefore Christ suffered in the flesh, arm yourselves with the same way of thinking, for whoever has suffered in the flesh has ceased from sin, so as to live for the rest of the time in the flesh no longer for human passions but for the will of God. For the time that is past suffices for doing what the Gentiles want to do, living in sensuality, passions, drunkenness, orgies, drinking parties, and lawless idolatry. With respect to this they are surprised when you do not join them in the same flood of debauchery, and they malign you; but they will give account to him who is ready to judge the living and the dead. For this is why the gospel was preached even to those who are dead, that though judged in the flesh the way people are, they might live in the spirit the way God does."

1 Peter 4:1-6

Jesus paid a price for our sins. His death was an atoning sacrifice. First Peter 4:1 commands, "Since therefore Christ suffered in the flesh, arm yourselves with the same way of thinking." "Arm yourself" is a technical, military term that means *get ready for battle*. Put your armor on. As we said yesterday, brace yourself.

Jesus willed Himself to be our sacrifice.

How did Jesus arm Himself for suffering? In the Gospels He always pointed out, "My time has not yet come" (John 7:6). Jesus knew from moment A where this was all going to lead. Forget that faulty idea that Jesus "ended up on the cross." He was in perfect control of every situation at every moment. Of course, Jesus could have called "legions of angels" (Matt. 26:53) to rescue Him, but Jesus *went* to the cross. He turned His face to Jerusalem and headed there (see Luke 9:51). Knowing exactly what was waiting for Him there, He went anyway. Jesus willed Himself to be our sacrifice.

Read the following Scripture passages and record what they reveal about Jesus' armed mind.

Matthew 4:3-4: *resisted*

Matthew 4:5-7: *Satan could not sway him*

Matthew 4:8-10:

John 4:31-32:

John 11:40-44:

Arm Yourself

When we face trials, we need to arm ourselves with the same mentality Jesus had. Instead of questioning why we are going through this trial, our mind-set must be: *I'm going to get through this trial. I'm not surprised by it. God has planned this trial for me, so I'm staying under it!*

Check the statements that demonstrate an armed mind-set toward suffering.

☐ Where's the door? I'm out of here!

☒ God knows I need this even if I can't see it.

☒ Bring it on, Lord. I know we can overcome this challenge.

☐ Why this? Why me? Why now?

☒ When the going gets tough, the tough get serious about trusting God.

☒ Thanks, Lord, for helping me understand in a small way what You went through for me in a big way.

How do you think the biblical truths you have examined in this study are arming you for current and future trials?

Resist Sin

Today's Scripture focus continues, "Whoever has suffered in the flesh has ceased from sin" (1 Pet. 4:1). This verse doesn't mean we won't sin when we're suffering. We can put that one in the wish-it-were-true category. Sadly, the opposite is more likely the case. Often when we're going through difficult times, we are more vulnerable to sin.

> We need to arm ourselves with the same mentality Jesus had.

A better translation of this verse conveys the idea of being restrained. It means when you suffer, God wants your suffering to restrain your sin—to make you a better Christian. He wants to use this trial in you life. Though temptation to sin can sometimes be heightened during trials, trials can make you more focused on your walk with Christ. Trials can sensitize you and even inoculate you against sin. The temptations may be greater, but so can your capacity for resistance.

As I look back through my journal over the past year of illness and cancer treatments, I notice that a seriousness has come into my spiritual life. If there were things in my life that I was not proud of, they came to light. When you suffer, pain in one area can sensitize you to what God is doing in other areas of life. Suffering teaches you that life isn't a series of random, unrelated events; it's all connected. As you formulate urgent prayer requests during your trial, you learn to examine your life for anything that would prevent your prayers from being heard: "OK, God. Is there anything You see in my life that I need to deal with? Anything that I need to get right with You about? Any subject that I've not been listening to You about?" When you intentionally seek to avoid sin during your trial, you develop the mind-set of a warrior who doesn't want to carry anything extra into the battle.

Read 2 Timothy 2:3:

"Share in suffering as a good soldier of Christ Jesus."

Does your prayer life indicate that you are armed and dangerous as Satan's enemy? ☐ Yes ☑ No

Is a trial making it harder or easier to walk closely with God? Why?

easier – I need him more

Guard Your Behavior

Today's Scripture focus says during a trial we must arm ourselves and resist sin. Why? "So as to live for the rest of the time in the flesh no longer for human passions but for the will of God" (I Pet. 4:2). It's talking about guarding our behavior. To a great extent, guarding our behavior sets the course of our lives. In what direction are you headed? God forgive us for the months and the years we spent with our pleasure at the top of our agenda. What a shallow existence that was. Instead of pursuing personal passions, go hard after the will of God. You may be in a trial that was particularly designed to steer you toward a pursuit of God's will.

> You may be in a trial that was particularly designed to steer you toward a pursuit of God's will.

If you are going through a trial, is it driving you to seek God's will in a deeper way? If so, how?

Trying to see the lesson

God's will is God's Word. Has your trial caused you to spend more time in the Word? If not, start searching it to find God's direction for your life during this hard time.

Stand Apart

Doing God's will includes refusing to do what the world wants you to do. Look at the next instruction in today's Scripture focus: "The time that is past suffices for doing what the Gentiles want to do, living in sensuality, passions, drunkenness, orgies, drinking parties, and lawless idolatry. With respect to this they are surprised when you do not join them in the same flood of debauchery, and they malign you; but they will give account to him who is ready to judge the living and the dead" (I Pet. 4:3-5).

"Doing what the Gentiles want to do" (v. 3) refers to the practices of a pagan life without Christ. Only foolish Christians would look back to their B.C. (Before Christ) days and want to keep doing those things. Peter listed some of those sins. One is "living in sensuality" (v. 3). The word *sensuality* means *a flagrant, unrestrained sexuality; no boundaries; no shame.* He also included "passions, drunkenness, orgies, drinking parties" (v. 3). The terms don't mean just sexual sin, though they definitely include that. Peter was referring to feasts at which people would stuff themselves with food, then make themselves vomit so that they could eat more. And then repeat. Then abuse alcohol and vomit. And then repeat. Any pathetic memories coming to mind? Then notice the summary term "lawless idolatry" (v. 3). The pagans used all of these practices in worshiping false gods; they were part of their religion.

Maybe you're thinking, *I would never do that.* Well, the modern-day god is *you.* We do all of these things in worshiping ourselves. We don't need a contest to discover the American Idol—it's each of us!

The modern-day god is *you.*

How do people practice self-worship today?

workaholic
keep up with Jones

Verse 4 takes on special significance in the context of suffering: "With respect to this they are surprised when you do not join them in the same flood of debauchery." The word *flood* carries the idea of being washed away by sin to a sudden, certain damnation. It's a flood of wickedness that rushes people into hell. No wonder Peter tells us to guard our behavior.

Those who don't go with the flow of debauchery are singled out for special treatment: "they malign you" (v. 4). The Greek word literally means they not only insult you but also blaspheme you: "Bible Thumper, Holy Roller, Jesus freak!" Yes, I am!

Read 1 Peter 4:5:

> "They will give account to him who is ready
> to judge the living and the dead."

What is waiting for people who malign believers who take a stand for Christ?

eternal life

Have you ever been persecuted for being a Christian? ☐ **Yes** ☑ **No**

What does your answer indicate about the degree to which your life stands out from the lives of unbelievers?

Are there any practices you need to repent of? Confess any sin and ask God to help you guard your behavior.

When it comes to joining the "flood of debauchery," I've been there, done that. Just shame and regret, heartache and devastation in that ride. I don't want any more of that in my life. If I'm going to suffer, let it be for good and for Christ! Arm yourself, resist sin, guard your behavior, and stand apart so that your life will be aligned with God's will. Then when you face a trial, you will be in a position for God to bring good from even the most difficult situation.

If I'm going to suffer, let it be for good and for Christ!

Day 3

GRACE YOUR RELATIONSHIPS

Today's Scripture Focus

"The end of all things is at hand; therefore be self-controlled and sober-minded for the sake of your prayers. Above all, keep loving one another earnestly, since love covers a multitude of sins. Show hospitality to one another without grumbling. As each has received a gift, use it to serve one another, as good stewards of God's varied grace: whoever speaks, as one who speaks oracles of God; whoever serves, as one who serves by the strength that God supplies—in order that in everything God may be glorified through Jesus Christ. To him belong glory and dominion forever and ever. Amen."

1 Peter 4:7-11

Peter has a way of keeping the end in front of our faces. In yesterday's passage he issued warnings about the way we are to live "the rest of the time in the flesh" (1 Pet. 4:2). In today's passage he points out that "the end of all things is at hand" (v. 7). Peter isn't asking us to get frantic; he is insisting that Jesus wants us to live each day as if it were the last before we meet Him face-to-face. One strategy for living with trials is to remember that there is an expiration date on life this side of eternity. Even if we have to endure trials for the rest of our time here, that time will come to an end. Then we will rest in God's presence.

Be Self-Controlled and Sober-Minded

In light of the fact that the end is coming, Peter instructs us to "be self-controlled and sober-minded for the sake of your prayers" (v. 7). We live in serious times. This is life and death. This is heaven and hell. This is about God's glory and Satan's kingdom in this world. This is about light and darkness. This is serious business. So when suffering comes to you, be self-controlled and sober-minded. Pain can sweep away shallowness and inattentiveness. Pain creates focus. Trials require that we respond, not based on the feeling of the moment but on self-control and ongoing reliance on God through prayer.

Pain creates focus.

What do self-controlled and sober-minded look like as you face a trial?

Love One Another

Then Peter says, "Above all, keep loving one another earnestly" (I Pet. 4:8). This is an above-all issue because our tendency is to become self-absorbed and irritable when we suffer. Love can be challenging when you're hurting. But in the middle of your trial when all of your energy is going into just trying to make it through another day, Peter says you need to love other people.

I love that word *earnestly*. When you are with the people you treasure, you want to take hold of them and love them earnestly. You are going to put some energy into it.

When have you most recently graced someone with earnest love?

Are you finding it difficult to express love in the middle of a trial? What makes it challenging?

Why does Peter tell us to love earnestly? Because "love covers a multitude of sins" (v. 8). If you love people, you don't want to shame them by repeating their deeds to others. You don't parade their problems for everyone to see. Even as you recount some of your trials, don't go into details that would hurt the people you love. You cover those things from view. Of course, if something illegal is going on, call the police. Hiding sin isn't biblical, and suffering abuse isn't spiritual. The authority structure in the church is meant to protect you when the authority structure in the home fails. But apart from an illegality, love covers; it protects.

Show Hospitality

One of the best ways to yield to God's will during a trial is to intentionally focus on the needs of others.

Today's Scripture focus also says to "show hospitality to one another without grumbling" (I Pet. 4:9). When you are consumed by a trial, it's easy to forget others and their needs. But Peter says one of the best ways to yield to God's will during a trial is to intentionally focus on the needs of others.

Check something you would like to do to show hospitality, even as you deal with hardship.

☐ **Have a party.**

☐ **Greet people as they enter the church building.**

- ☐ **Prepare a meal for someone.**

- ☐ **Invite someone over who is lonely.**

- ☐ **Take a gift to a new church member.**

- ☐ **Take a treat to someone who is discouraged.**

- ☐ **Write a note to someone who is enduring a trial.**

- ☐ **Other:**

Use Your Gift

First Peter 4:10 says, "As each has received a gift, use it to serve one another." Every follower of Jesus Christ has been given a spiritual gift, a supernatural enabling from the Holy Spirit. I believe that you get at least one gift. But think of it like a pie. I got a big slice of leadership, a medium-sized piece of administration, another piece of exhortation, and a thin slice of mercy in my pie. You might say, "Oh! I've got a great big piece of mercy." Our pies are unique, with combinations of several ingredients. This is your gift, and God gave it to you to serve Him.

> **Take a few minutes to reflect on your spiritual gift. What capacities and abilities seem to make up the gift God's Spirit has placed in you? Read Romans 12:6-8; 1 Corinthians 12:8-10,28; and Ephesians 4:11 and think about the percentages of gifts that make up your pie. You might also want to ask someone else to tell you what they think your spiritual gift is. Then draw lines in the circle to represent the components of your gift.**

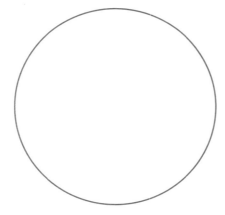

It's not enough to identify your spiritual gift. Peter admonishes you to use it to serve others. This is especially important when you or someone you know is experiencing a trial. Your own trials can sensitize you to the needs of others. Trials also help you learn how to use your spiritual gift to help and encourage others who are hurting.

Trials help you learn how to use your spiritual gift to help and encourage others who are hurting.

When You Speak

Just a word of warning: if you think your gift is encouragement, be very submissive to the Lord when you talk to someone in a trial. If people see you coming across the church parking lot and quickly duck in their car and race off, that's probably not your gift. Everyone who has been through a trial could tell you about somebody who said something that hurt. Thoughtless words, intended to encourage, can add significant pain.

Then what do you say to someone undergoing a trial? First Peter 4:11 says, "... whoever speaks, as one who speaks the oracles of God." The oracles of God are the words of God, that is, Scripture. You will never go wrong sharing Scripture with someone who is hurting. Avoid passages that are judgmental; instead, share verses that meant a lot to you when you were suffering. Pour God's amazing grace into someone's life directly from His Word. Send a verse in the mail or by e-mail: "Dear John: Praying for you. Reference. Verse. Love, your name." God's Word will feed and bless the person. You can be a messenger to let this person know that God is in charge of the trial and that He is available to help.

Verse 11 continues, "... whoever serves, as one who serves by the strength that God supplies." After you share Scripture, use your gift. If you're a server, serve. If you're a speaker, speak. But whatever you do, do it "by the strength that God supplies." Be prayed up. Be filled with the Spirit. If you want to be used to bless someone who's going through a trial, you need to be right with God. You need to be drawing from God's strength. You need to be praying, "Lord, give me wisdom to know how I can help."

> **Even if you are going through a trial, think of three persons you know who could use encouragement from Scripture. Write their names on the left and ask God for a verse for each of them. E-mail or write to them today.**
>
> **Names**   **Verses**
>
> **1.**
>
> **2.**
>
> **3.**

Paul gave the Colossians great counsel: "Let your speech always be gracious, seasoned with salt, so that you may know how you ought to answer each person" (Col. 4:6). Ask God to give you His grace today—grace for your trial and for your ministry to someone else who is hurting. The test of His grace in our lives is how plain that grace is to others when we are going through trials.

You will never go wrong sharing Scripture with someone who is hurting.

Day 4

GLORIFY YOUR GOD

Today's Scripture Focus

"Beloved, do not be surprised at the fiery trial when it comes upon you
to test you, as though something strange were happening to you.
But rejoice insofar as you share Christ's sufferings, that you may
also rejoice and be glad when his glory is revealed. If you are insulted
for the name of Christ, you are blessed, because the Spirit of glory and
of God rests upon you. But let none of you suffer as a murderer or a thief
or an evildoer or as a meddler. Yet if anyone suffers as a Christian,
let him not be ashamed, but let him glorify God in that name."

1 Peter 4:12-16

Yesterday's passage ended with a short benediction: "… in order that in everything God may be glorified through Jesus Christ. To him belong glory and dominion forever and ever. Amen" (1 Pet. 4:11). That thought carries over into our challenge today as we continue learning what to do with trials. Peter says when we face a "fiery trial," we should not be surprised but "rejoice and be glad when his glory is revealed" (vv. 12-13). If Peter had been using modern picture language, he might have written, "Make sure the default setting in your life is to glorify God."

Make sure the default setting in your life is to glorify God.

What are some ways Christians glorify God?

How do we glorify God through our trials?

We Have Seen His Glory

When we talk about glorifying God, we don't mean we're adding to His glory. His glory is not a fading brightness that we can pump up by doing something. Often, glorifying God actually means getting out of the way so that someone else can see Him more clearly!

Glory emanates from God. Remember Moses' bold request in Exodus 33:18-23? Moses asked to see God, but God responded, "You can't. My glory would wipe you out. But I'll tell you what: hide in this rock. I'll pass by, and then you can see My afterburn. If you actually saw Me, you'd burn." You can't see God and live. All you see is His glory, the manifestation of His presence, the evidence that He's around.

That unmistakable presence is what the disciples sensed when they were with Jesus. John reported, "The Word became flesh and dwelt among us, and we have seen his glory, glory as of the only Son from the Father, full of grace and truth" (John 1:14). Many memorable moments when Jesus was flesh and dwelled among us occurred during His trials and suffering. In the way Jesus handled living and dying, the disciples saw glory. And if you know Jesus, you have also seen His glory. In everything that happens to us, even trials, our continued decision to honor Christ will allow others to see His glory as well.

> **In everything that happens to us, even trials, our continued decision to honor Christ will allow others to see His glory.**

Identify a time when you saw God's glory in some way.

When Kathy and I were staying in California while I was undergoing cancer treatments, we took a walk every morning in the hills near our rental. We remarked every day about how beautiful the mountains were. The psalmist asked:

> "I lift up my eyes to the hills.
> From where does my help come?" *Psalm 121:1*

The answer follows:

> "My help comes from the LORD,
> who made heaven and earth." *Psalm 121:2*

The psalmist looked at creation and thought, *God!* Creation is shouting God's name and God's glory (see Ps. 19). He created the universe to glorify Himself. Those moments in the hills were little breathers from the cancer treatments. The hills put my present trial in perspective.

What part of creation most speaks to you about God's glory? Why?

The interesting point is that the voice of creation will always be muted. The defining moment of creation is humankind. Like the rest of creation, we are here to display God's glory. Jesus said, "If these [his disciples] were silent, the very stones would cry out" (Luke 19:40). The message of God's existence cannot be silenced in the universe. The evidence of God's presence can't be entirely avoided.

You are here to show God's presence to everyone around you. That's what your life is about. You probably knew this before, but now for sure you won't forget that I told you. This is what your life is about going forward. You can say to yourself with confidence, *I am here to display the superiority of a life lived in God. I'm here to do what the mountains do very poorly. My life is to shout the existence of God.* And that is no less true when you go through trials. The way you handle your hardship can tell people around you that your hope is in the Lord as they observe, "Look at the way she goes through these trials. Look at the way he triumphs no matter what! God must be in his life!" Yes, He is. That's why you are here—to glorify God. And the fact that at any time trials may consume part or all of life doesn't let you off the hook. In suffering you can glorify God.

> The way you handle your hardship can tell people around you that your hope is in the Lord.

Living on Display

When we think, *I am here to display the superiority of a life lived in God,* our first thought may be sheer panic. It is not an announcement we are going to declare to a crowded room. But it must be a continual reminder of what should drive our lives. So how do we live in a way that glorifies God? Our constant aim should be to live according to God's Word, which we have already discovered is the equivalent of living according to His will. When we are in tune with His instructions, God will have the opportunity to alert others about His glory.

We must resist the urge (in easy or hard times) to try to glorify God by meeting other people's expectations. They won't always get it when we praise God in our trials. It's surprising how often others will bring God into a conversation first, if only to question why we are not blaming Him for our circumstances. The discouraging but predictable human tendency is to practice the approach of Job's wife to the difficulties others are facing: "His wife said to him, 'Do you still hold fast your integrity? Curse God and die'" (Job 2:9). We can excuse her vehemence due to her own extreme grief, but her statement illustrates how others can encourage us to question God even when we are doing our best to give Him glory. Some people will be baffled if they don't hear us complaining against God when we are in trials. They expect us to join them in resentment against Him. Our refusal to hold God responsible may not go over well. We may even find that people who commiserate with us one moment will turn on us in the next and accuse us of unrealistic confidence in Christ. That is part of what Peter means by "If you are insulted for the name of Christ ..." (1 Pet. 4:14).

Apply the statement "I am here to display the superiority of a life lived in God" to the following areas.

I am here to display the superiority of a life lived in God in my (choose one):
☐ **marriage**   ☐ **work**   ☐ **friendships by:**

I am here to display the superiority of a life lived in God in my (choose one):
☐ **trials**   ☐ **adversity**   ☐ **suffering by:**

Is your life bringing glory to God even as you face a trial?   ☐ **Yes**   ☐ **No**

If so, in what ways?

Take your calendar in hand and offer it in prayer to God. Tell Him you understand that the dates and appointments on these pages are your plans for using time He still hasn't officially given you. Declare that you want your use of time to glorify Him. Pray the words of the psalmist, who wrote,

"My times are in your hand." *Psalm 31:15*

Ask God to help you glorify Him even when you face trials.

Suffering as a Christian

Today's Scripture focus specifically addresses suffering for the name of Christ: "If you are insulted for the name of Christ, you are blessed, because the Spirit of glory and of God rests upon you. But let none of you suffer as a murderer or a thief or an evildoer or as a meddler. Yet if anyone suffers as a Christian, let him not be ashamed, but let him glorify God in that name" (I Pet. 4:14-16). Suffering for Christ can be shocking to us because we don't expect people to retaliate when we try to treat them with genuine love. *Persecution* is an ugly word; yet believers all around the world frequently suffer for the name of Christ. In the United States we have to ask, *Is the fact that we are not suffering persecution because our nation is a haven for Christianity or because we aren't really living enough like Christians to merit a backlash?*

Have you suffered for Christ? How?

If someone were targeting Christians for persecution, what would be the primary evidence against you?

In what ways are you prepared to suffer for Christ in the future?

Like all trials, persecution is not an experience we relish, but Peter indicates that those who suffer for the name of Christ are blessed. Fellow believers in other parts of the world are suffering for Christ every day, and we should pray for them. And we should pray that if God allows this kind of trial to come our way, we will "rejoice and be glad" to share in Christ's sufferings (I Pet. 4:13).

Those who suffer for the name of Christ are blessed.

Day 5
WHAT TO DO

Today's Scripture Focus

"It is time for judgment to begin at the household of God;
and if it begins with us, what will be the outcome for those
who do not obey the gospel of God? And
'If the righteous is scarcely saved,
what will become of the ungodly and the sinner?'
"Therefore let those who suffer according to God's will entrust
their souls to a faithful Creator while doing good."

1 Peter 4:17-19

Tucked among yesterday's and today's verses are four *whats* we can do before, during, and after trials. As we live our lives, we ought to constantly rotate among these actions like a circuit of apparatuses in a spiritual exercise gym. Each one of these four actions is a shortcut to giving glory to God.

What to Do: Rejoice

Peter would have given a loud "Amen!" to Paul's familiar command "Rejoice in the Lord always; again I will say, Rejoice" (Phil. 4:4). Peter didn't hesitate to include times of suffering in his definition of *always:* "Rejoice insofar as you share Christ's sufferings, that you may also rejoice and be glad when his glory is revealed" (1 Pet. 4:13). If I'm living for God's glory, His glory will ultimately be revealed.

"When his glory is revealed" (v. 13) applies not only in an ultimate sense but also in the ongoing progression of your trial as God's glory becomes apparent. If you submit to His discipline and allow Him to do His work through your trial, you won't be able to help yourself; you will rejoice. Even though the trial may not be over, seeing a glimpse of God's glory in the middle of it will make you rejoice as nothing else can.

> **Even though the trial may not be over, seeing a glimpse of God's glory in the middle of it will make you rejoice.**

In the middle of chaotic circumstances and difficult times, it is helpful to remember what doesn't change. We can rejoice over changing and temporary things, but a more dependable starting point is always what we know about God that is unchangeable.

A friend of mine repeats a line from an old song to help him keep rejoicing. He hums, whistles, or sings, "He never sleeps; He never slumbers" to remind himself that God watches over him at every moment. What unchangeable things about God have that effect on you? What aspects of God's character or which of His promises are certain every morning for you? List at least five traits or promises of God that would make you rejoice even in hard times.

1.

2.

3.

4.

5.

What to Do: Don't Be Ashamed

Yesterday's Scripture focus included this sentence: "If anyone suffers as a Christian, let him not be ashamed" (1 Pet. 4:16). Don't be ashamed if you suffer hardship because you love God, because you won't lower the flag, because you won't give up, because you won't stop talking about Him. Manifest the reality of God's presence in your life. Remember to have the mind Jesus had when He "endured the cross, despising the shame" (Heb. 12:2). He had the same mind before it all began when He "made himself nothing, taking the form of a servant" (see Phil. 2:5-11).

This gets to the center of what it means to entrust ourselves to Christ. We can't depend on Him as Savior or obey Him as Lord if at heart we are ashamed of Him. Jesus said, "Whoever is ashamed of me and of my words in this adulterous and sinful generation, of him will the Son of Man also be ashamed when he comes in the glory of his Father with the holy angels" (Mark 8:38). If you aren't sold out to Jesus in times of peace, are you going to be able to stand up for Him under persecution?

> If you aren't sold out to Jesus in times of peace, are you going to be able to stand up for Him under persecution?

Although your life probably isn't being threatened, maybe there are times when you hesitate to speak the truth about Jesus. Check any reason(s) you are giving in to shame, even in seemingly small ways.

☐ **Speaking up might bring humiliation or rejection.**

☐ **I don't want to get involved with someone who is antagonistic.**

☐ **I don't want to take the time to present what I believe about Christ.**

☐ **I'm afraid I will be ridiculed at work or in the community.**

☐ **Other:**

Begin looking for opportunities to share ways God has strengthened your faith through the hard times you have experienced. Pray that your Heavenly Father will help you trust Him enough to speak up and to leave the consequences to Him.

What to Do: Self-Exam

Today's Scripture focus warns, "It is time for judgment to begin at the household of God; and if it begins with us, what will be the outcome for those who do not obey the gospel of God?" (1 Pet. 4:17). Peter is challenging us to prepare for God's judgment by looking at our own lives. Instead of judging nonbelievers, we should ask ourselves how we are doing as God's children who understand what He expects of us.

And if that didn't make us uncomfortable enough, Peter continues, "If the righteous is scarcely saved, what will become of the ungodly and the sinner?" (v. 18). One of the good things about trials is that if we submit to them as opportunities to learn from God, they can make us realize that we are completely dependent on Him. Grace doesn't just save us; grace keeps us. We couldn't take the first step without God, and we can't take any other steps without Him. We can't do anything right spiritually without Him. And we can't be successful in trials without Him.

> The point of a self-examination is to be truthful with ourselves about the way we practice following Jesus.

It's all about grace. That's what Peter means by "scarcely saved" (v. 18). We're just hanging on by the grace of God. If a self-exam doesn't leave us quiet, broken, and humble before God, it wasn't an effective self-exam. We need to do it over. The point of a self-examination is to be truthful with ourselves about the way we practice following Jesus. If we don't realize our complete dependence on God's grace, we are taking salvation for granted. The same is true of our trial. If it hasn't led us to a point of surrender to God's discipline, we haven't learned what He intended for us to learn through this experience.

Time for a self-exam. Begin by praying:

> "Search me, O God, and know my heart!
> Try me and know my thoughts!
> And see if there be any grievous way in me,
> and lead me in the way everlasting!"
> *Psalm 139:23-24*

Ask God to show you whether you are living totally by His grace or still trying to hold on and do things in your own power. Has your trial led you to a point of brokenness and dependence on Him that you haven't known before? If so, thank Him for His grace and for the shaping He is doing through His loving discipline. If not, admit your dependence on Him and ask for His grace to learn what He wants to teach you through this trial.

What to Do: Entrust

Peter's fourth *what* sounds a note of encouragement: "Let those who suffer according to God's will entrust their souls to a faithful Creator while doing good" (1 Pet. 4:19). It's as if Peter is pulling us close together and saying, "I know you're suffering. Don't quit. Don't give up. Don't stop teaching your class. Don't stop leading your small group. Don't stop sharing your faith. Don't stop reading your Bible. Keep going in the midst of trials. Keep being faithful."

Above all, entrust your soul to your faithful Creator. God is faithful, He is in control, and He is good. Decide now that you're going to trust Him as you wait until the darkness becomes light.

Exuberant rejoicing, shameless allegiance, and fearless self-examination demand that we take up our cross and follow Jesus even when we don't feel like it. Ultimately, your relationship with God is not performance based. It is grace and trust based. As you walk through your trial, are you entrusting your soul to your faithful Creator? ☐ **Yes** ☐ **No Explain your answer.**

Entrust your soul to your faithful Creator.

WHAT IF I REFUSE THIS TRIAL?

This Week's Scripture Focus

"Lift your drooping hands and strengthen your weak knees, and make straight paths for your feet, so that what is lame may not be put out of joint but rather be healed. Strive for peace with everyone, and for the holiness without which no one will see the Lord. See to it that no one fails to obtain the grace of God; that no 'root of bitterness' springs up and causes trouble, and by it many become defiled; that no one is sexually immoral or unholy like Esau, who sold his birthright for a single meal. For you know that afterward, when he desired to inherit the blessing, he was rejected, for he found no chance to repent, though he sought it with tears."
Hebrews 12:12-17

The Narrow Way

Although no two persons live identical lives, they may have gone through similar circumstances. And yet the outcomes of two parallel lives can be radically different. People can respond in almost directly opposite ways to hardship. One can end up bitter, the other better! Suffering can produce attractive tenderness in one and rock hardness in another. It is not far from the mark to say that 10 percent of life is what happens to you, and 90 percent is how you deal with the 10 percent.

We have emphasized throughout this study that none of us get through life without suffering. In fact, as followers of Jesus, we fully expect to suffer. God's Word provides several sources of guidance when we suffer. First, we have Jesus' example. He walked the Via Dolorosa, the way of suffering, on our behalf and as our example. Though that way was painful, Jesus never flinched from his resolve to carry out the Father's will.

Second, the Bible clearly warns us that when we take wrong turns in life by rejecting God's discipline, we can expect to pass through some difficult lands that will either drive us farther away from the life we should be living or back to the narrow way, where we have fellowship with Christ. This week we will visit each of these lands to discover why we never want to go there.

Week 4
GROUP EXPERIENCE

As You Gather

1. **Suffering can be a difficult and tiring journey. Even though we have been looking for three weeks at the hard side of life, there have probably been some funny moments along the way for you. Share something you heard, saw, or felt during or between your group sessions that made you laugh.**

2. **What places in the world have you visited that you would not visit again? Why?**

Preparation and Review

1. **Based on last week's group session and workbook assignments, what would you say is one new addition to the arsenal of responses you can make when hard times come in life?**

2. **Describe how you are applying the insights from this study to a trial you are experiencing. Would you describe yourself as still stuck, going backward, or moving in the right direction?**

3. **As we prepare for this week's teaching, what are some of the results you would expect to see in the life of someone who rejects the trials God allows into his or her life?**

DVD Session 4 Viewer Guide

Trials can lead to _Discouragement_ **(see Heb. 12:12-13a).**

Discouragement can lead to _Dislocation_ **(see Heb. 12:13b-14).**

A trial is a painful circumstance allowed by God to change my _conduct_ and my _character_.

Holiness, the number one fruit in the life of a believer, is a longing desire to be more like Jesus Christ.

Dislocation can lead to _Bitterness_ (see Heb. 12:15).

Falling short of the grace in _salvation_ is trying to save yourself.

Falling short of the grace in _sanctification_ is trying to sanctify yourself.

Bitterness can lead to _profane living_
(see Heb. 12:16).

The things of _God_ didn't mean anything to Esau.

Profane living can lead to disqualification (see Heb. 12:17).

We pursue holiness not perfectly but _increasingly_.

Genuine repentance means to _change_ your mind.

Responding to the DVD Teaching

1. **Discuss the impact of this teaching on your response to trials.**

2. **Identify statements people use to justify or rationalize their response in each of the five stages presented on the DVD segment:**

   • Discouragement

   • Dislocation

   • Bitterness

   • Profane living

   • Disqualification

3. **What does _holiness_ mean? When have you made the most progress in holiness during your Christian life?**

Read week 4 and complete the activities before the next group experience.

If you missed this session, you can download the DVD teaching from _www.lifeway.com/downloads_.

Day 1
THE LAND OF DISCOURAGEMENT

Today's Scripture Focus

"Lift your drooping hands and strengthen your weak knees,
and make straight paths for your feet."

Hebrews 12:12-13

The first hazard sign you'll meet when you go through something difficult is a sense of discouragement. And that's why you see the admonishment in Hebrews 12:12 to "lift your drooping hands and strengthen your weak knees." Can you picture it? If someone comes your way with drooping hands and weak knees, they might as well be wearing a sign across their chest that reads, Discouraged. The command to lift and strengthen is, first of all, a word of hope. Discouragement leads us to the conclusion that we can't lift our hands or strengthen our knees. But if help comes from the outside, we can have hope.

Make Straight Paths

Of all the lands we will visit this week, discouragement is the one that most often sneaks up on us. The trip to low-spirits country is the shortest. One blink and you're there. Don't ignore the early signs of discouragement: listlessness, disinterest, sadness, and tiredness. When we prayerfully admit to God we're discouraged, He doesn't pile on; but we may still have to live with dismay and depression for a while until we have learned all He wants to teach us through this trial. After all, it has come for our good. Remember that a trial is a painful circumstance allowed by God to change our conduct and our character.

The writer of Hebrews also said to "make straight paths for your feet" (v. 13). When you're going through a trial, you don't have any time or energy for a walk in the park. You want to get as fast as you can from point A to point B. You want to keep everything simple. Yet discouragement tends to distract you from God's purposes, causing you to wander off the straight pathway. The command to make straight paths clearly speaks to someone who is discouraged yet is willing to remain under God's hand, saying, "I want to learn this, God!" Even in trials we have to press forward, step-by-step, meeting God as He moves toward us.

Discouragement tends to distract you from God's purposes.

Identify a time in the past when a trial left you in the land of discouragement.

Which of the following statements best describes the way you escaped from that country?

☐ An unexpected blessing overwhelmed my discouragement.

☐ I realized I had been ignoring God, and that started my healing.

☐ The immediate cause of my discouragement was removed or changed.

☐ I don't remember, but I sensed God's hand at work.

☐ I became more discouraged before I became better.

☐ Other:

Read Job 4:2-6. What did Eliphaz point out to Job that was ironic about Job's discouragement?

He was such a help to others

Why is this a good example of what not to say to someone who is discouraged?

Read Joshua 1:9:

> "Be strong and courageous. Do not be frightened, and do not be dismayed, for the LORD your God is with you wherever you go."

What is the primary reason we don't need to be discouraged?

We are not alone

We make straight paths during our trials when we recognize God's presence with us, His resources for our problems, and His purposes for working trials for our good. Our job is to remain under God's discipline to receive the benefit of our difficult circumstance.

Avoid Crooked Paths

But what about the person who doesn't want to learn from trials because of the discouragement? The one who cuts and runs? There are a number of ways to get lost on crooked paths when a trial has you discouraged.

Denial. Maybe you are in denial:

- "That's not my trial. God's not trying to teach me anything."

- "This isn't really happening. We don't have a problem in our marriage."

- "I'm not facing financial difficulty."

- "I'm not going to the doctor for tests. I'm going to be fine!"

Denial heightens discouragement.

Denial heightens discouragement because you can't be in partnership with God in something you're not acknowledging or accepting.

Finger-pointing. Maybe you're into finger-pointing: "Oh yeah, there's a problem. I don't deny it. And the problem is you!" That response only increases your discouragement because it cuts you off from potentially supportive relationships.

Shifting blame. Maybe shifting blame is your avoidance strategy: "Oh yeah, there's a problem. And fine, the problem's me. But it's not my fault. It's because of all of you people! You're all driving me crazy!"

These faulty attitudes often show up in the early stages of trials, but they only heighten discouragement in your life because you're not embracing what God has allowed to come into your life. You're not acknowledging that this trial is intended for your good.

Choose someone whose opinion you trust and describe the three faulty strategies (denial, finger-pointing, and shifting blame) for dealing with the discouragement of a trial. Ask this person if he or she has noticed your using any of those strategies. What did you learn?

Trials don't have to lead to discouragement. Any difficult season brings grief, but it doesn't have to linger. Today's Scripture focus says you can lift your drooping hands, strengthen your weak knees, and make straight paths for your feet. This means by accepting God's discipline and submitting to His loving work in your difficulty, you can heal. You can get better. You can get up. You can go on in God's strength.

If you are facing discouragement in living through a trial, take a few minutes to be quiet before God. Then entrust yourself to Him by verbally placing yourself in His care. Don't hurry. Declare your trust in Him beyond your feelings of discouragement.

Trials don't have to lead to discouragement.

Day 2
THE LAND OF DISLOCATION

Today's Scripture Focus

"Make straight paths for your feet, so that what is lame may not
be put out of joint but rather be healed. Strive for peace with everyone,
and for the holiness without which no one will see the Lord."

Hebrews 12:13-14

The discouragement we looked at yesterday is a problem; but if it isn't addressed, it can lead to dislocation, which is even worse. There are frequent flights from the land of discouragement into the land of dislocation.

Out of Joint

Today's Scripture focus says, "Make straight paths for your feet, so that what is lame may not be put out of joint but rather be healed" (v. 13). This verse describes God's children who are experiencing God's discipline as lame. You have a limp, and God is turning on the pressure. If you try to get out from under the pressure when it's still on, the angle of your joint creates an injury. And if your angle is that instead of submitting to God, you resist, rebel, and refuse His discipline, then you're going to get hurt!

It is pressure combined with the wrong angle that creates the injury. When you go up for a rebound in basketball and come down without having your feet back under you or land on someone else's foot, you're going down. All of your weight comes crashing down on the wrong side of your ankle, and you go right to the floor. If you're submitting to God and that pressure's coming down on you, He will give you strength to bear up under a lot more. But if you refuse to remain under it, you are out of alignment with His purposes for this time of discipline. When pressure is applied, your contorted angle creates pain.

Hebrews 12:13 calls this condition being "out of joint." The NIV translates it "disabled." The NKJV translates it "dislocated." It's one thing to have a sprained ankle; it's another thing to have a dislocated ankle. A dislocation is very serious.

> If you're submitting to God and that pressure's coming down on you, He will give you strength to bear up under a lot more.

Read Genesis 32:22-32. What led to Jacob's dislocation, and what led to his new name?

Is there any spiritual limping in your life? Are there past breaks that have healed, but the damage caused by your resistance to God's discipline has remained? To what degree have you submitted those lasting injuries to God for His care?

Are you resisting God's discipline at this present time? Are there any signs that you are in danger of dislocation?

Today's Scripture focus says God's goal in your trial is to heal what is lame. God doesn't want this trial to devastate your life. He wants it to cause just enough pain to get your attention and to convey the lesson "Get healed and go on to be the person God wants you to be. If you resist now, a more serious injury is coming."

> God's goal in your trial is to heal what is lame.

Strive for Peace and Holiness

A dislocated life doesn't have to be your fate. Hebrews 12:14 says to "strive for peace with everyone." With everyone? Maybe you're getting along fine with your family and your neighbors. But the verse says not just your favorite people but all people.

Many of us live in an undeclared state of war with certain people in our lives. When we do, we invite dislocation. What relationships would have to change for you to be at peace with everyone?

Hebrews 12:14 also tell us to strive "for the holiness without which no one will see the Lord." I've been teaching God's Word for 25 years. When you tell people to strive for holiness, they make the craziest face. You know why? Because they don't have a clue what holiness is. If they had more of it, they'd know how awesome it is. Sadly, most Christians treat God's desire to create holiness in their lives as if He were giving them cod-liver oil.

Holiness is fantastic. It's you operating according to the Manufacturer's specifications. Holiness is once and for all putting behind you the silly, on-the-surface posing and posturing that exalt yourself. Holiness is the soul-satisfying, saturating presence of God in your life. It is the air you were created to breathe!

> Holiness is the soul-satisfying, saturating presence of God in your life.

In the past what has been your attitude about holiness?

☐ **I didn't know I was supposed to be holy.**

☐ **I didn't know what holiness was.**

☐ **I wanted holiness but didn't know how to be holy.**

☐ **I knew what holiness was but didn't think it was important.**

☐ **Other:**

Holiness is essential, not optional. "Without holiness," verse 14 says, "no one will see the Lord" (NIV). Maybe your reaction is, *I thought all I had to do was turn from my sin, embrace Jesus Christ by faith, and be forgiven. Then I would go to heaven.* Yes, that's how you get on the salvation boat. But everybody who's really on the boat is fired up about holiness, not always perfectly but increasingly. They're fired up about holiness because if you get more, you want more! That's what holiness is like. That's what James 2:26 means when it says, "Faith apart from works is dead." Works don't save you, but the people who have saving faith perform good works. If your faith hasn't changed you, it hasn't saved you. So real saving faith results in works, fruit, and a desire for holiness.

Mark a spot on the continuum to rate your current level of desire for holiness.

●───●

Low   **High**

If your desire for holiness is low, what do you think is holding you back?

What areas of your life have you kept as God-free zones that you control?

In what sense is your reluctance to pursue holiness creating a feeling of dislocation between you and God?

Relocating a joint can be as painful as the original dislocation. The same is true of spiritual dislocation. Surrendering to God in an area in which we have been resisting His work may involve a certain discomfort or pain. But striving for peace and holiness is the way we are to remain under God's loving hand and to see Him at work in our painful circumstances. The assurance that God desires us to be in a right relationship with Him will eventually make the pain worthwhile!

Ask God to show you any ways you are resisting His work and suffering dislocation. Ask for His healing as you submit to His discipline through this trial in your life.

> Striving for peace and holiness is the way we are to remain under God's loving hand and to see Him at work in our painful circumstances.

Day 3

THE LAND OF BITTERNESS

Today's Scripture Focus

"See to it that no one fails to obtain the grace of God; that no 'root of bitterness' springs up and causes trouble, and by it many become defiled."
Hebrews 12:15

If you get a serious injury from dislocation and still don't accept the trial in your life, you have decided not to be trained by it. If you refuse to say, "God, as painful as this is, I know it's from You, and I want to get the good out of it," you're well on your way to the land of bitterness.

Obtain Grace

Today's Scripture focus includes an important admonition for anyone going through a trial: "See to it that no one fails to obtain the grace of God" (Heb. 12:15). What does that mean? Galatians 5:4 explains, "You have become estranged by Christ, you who attempt to be justified by the law; you have fallen from grace" (NKJV). Falling short of grace in salvation is you trying to save you. Falling short of grace in sanctification is trying to sanctify yourself or take charge of your spiritual life. God puts a trial in your life, and instead of submitting to the trial and placing yourself under His discipline, you resist and rebel and refuse the trial. You fight against it. You fail to obtain the grace of God through the circumstance He has allowed in your life for your sanctification.

> **This verse in Hebrews says not to fail "to obtain the grace of God." The word *obtain* usually implies a search or an effort on your part. But if you don't have to earn God's grace, how do you obtain His grace during a trial?**

If you're just surviving, you're not getting the grace of God.

If you aren't getting God's grace during a trial, you might be faking it, white-knuckling it, trying to gut it out, telling yourself, *Hang on, Man! We're going to get through this!* But you're not walking with God. You're not digging into His Word. You're not praying. You're not admitting your helplessness and submitting to God's good purposes. You're not turning up the volume on the spiritual dials in your soul. If you're just surviving, you're not getting the grace of God.

Or maybe you're putting on the hypersubmission act: "Go ahead, God! Where's the steamroller? Just go ahead and run me over!" Trials don't accomplish their beneficial work when you respond with a victim mentality.

> **Describe a time (maybe right now) when you have approached a trial by white-knuckling it or by being hypersubmissive. What do these two approaches have in common that guarantees their failure?**

Trying to gut it out or being hypersubmissive might sound spiritual, but neither approach is a partnership with God. Both of those extremes miss the grace of God for your trial.

A Bitter Root

People going through hard times often ask, "How can I know if I'm responding the wrong way?" Hebrews 12:15 tells us, "See to it that no one fails to obtain the grace of God; that no 'root of bitterness' springs up and causes trouble, and by it many become defiled." Deuteronomy 29:18-19 gives a similar warning: "Beware lest there be among you a root bearing poisonous and bitter fruit." Moses wasn't talking about a plant; he was talking about a poisonous person. Then he gave a profile of a bitter person: "One who, when he hears the words of this sworn covenant, blesses himself in his heart, saying, 'I shall be safe, though I walk in the stubbornness of my heart.' "

That's a bitter person. When a trial comes, this person says, "I don't want it! I hear what the Word of God says. I understand it, but I go on with life because I think I will be safe, though I walk in the stubbornness of my heart. I don't care what you say! I don't care what the Bible says! I'm never going to be happy about this thing that's happened to me! Don't ask me to try to find joy about this! I refuse to be happy about it!"

> **Have you ever visited the land of bitterness? Do you live there now? Describe the cause of your bitterness and your attitude toward the trial that led you there.**

Someone in the Bible who struggled with bitterness was Naomi, Ruth's mother-in-law and mentor. Read Naomi's statement when she returned husbandless and childless from a decade away in Moab:

> "The two of them [Naomi and Ruth] went on until they came to Bethlehem. And when they came to Bethlehem, the whole town was stirred because of them. And the women said, 'Is this Naomi?' She said to them, 'Do not call me Naomi; call me Mara [meaning *bitter*], for the Almighty has dealt very bitterly with me. I went away full, and the LORD has brought me back empty. Why call me Naomi, when the LORD has testified against me and the Almighty has brought calamity upon me?' "
>
> *Ruth 1:19-21*

How did Naomi respond to the suffering she had experienced?

Later, through an amazing sequence of events, Ruth met and married Boaz and presented Naomi with a grandchild. Naomi hung in there and experienced God's grace! Her friends expressed the blessing that had come to Naomi by saying:

> " 'Blessed be the LORD, who has not left you this day without a redeemer, and may his name be renowned in Israel! He shall be to you a restorer of life and a nourisher of your old age, for your daughter-in-law who loves you, who is more to you than seven sons, has given birth to him.' Then Naomi took the child and laid him on her lap and became his nurse."
>
> *Ruth 4:14-16*

God didn't want Naomi to stay in the land of bitterness. He used events and people to bring her out of bitterness and into a new day of blessing and hope.

If you are bitter about your trial, everyone who knows and loves you is so ready for you to change. What's more bitter than living with a bitter person? God's Word warns you not to let a "root of bitterness" spring up and cause trouble (Heb. 12:15). When a toxic mixture of anger and disappointment enters your heart, it wraps around your soul, clouding your judgment and distorting the way you see everything.

It doesn't have to be that way. I know people who have been through the darkest, most unimaginable series of difficult things—not just one thing but three or four or five tragedies that shouldn't happen to one person. Instead of feeling bitter,

When a toxic mixture of anger and disappointment enters your heart, it wraps around your soul, clouding your judgment and distorting the way you see everything.

they have the sweetest heart for the Lord, and it shows in everything they do. In their soul grows a root of tenderness.

I know other people who have been through a lot less and are cold, calloused, and twisted. They have a root of bitterness. And if you think the root's ugly, wait until you see the ugly tree. Hebrews 12:15 says " 'a root of bitterness' springs up." If the root is there because you have refused God's grace for your hardship, it's going to grow into a tree! Your attitude toward the trial that God has allowed might be a secret for a while, but it's not going to be a secret forever. Eventually, it's coming out. When that bitterness comes out, it "springs up and causes trouble, and by it many become defiled." *Defiled* is the word translated *torment* in Luke 6:18. It's what demons do to people. Can you imagine how destructive that kind of defilement is to your heart?

How can bitterness defile your heart?

How can bitterness defile people around you?

Bitterness begins when God allows a trial to come into your life, and you don't like your circumstances. Perhaps He has not allowed you to have children; you can't find a job; or you experience a loss, an injury, or an illness. Instead of accepting that God in His wisdom has allowed this trial for your benefit and that He's appointed to you a season of adversity, you respond, "I don't want it! I refuse it! I deeply resent it!" Discouragement becomes dislocation when you try to get out from under the discipline, and you are injured. Then instead of getting humble, you get bitter. Bitterness defiles many people. It ruins marriages and children. It ruins the love and the joy in a church.

Bitterness starts out as a root, but it grows into a tree. If you have reached the land of bitterness, make sure you deal with it now by submitting to God's purpose for your trial. He's allowed it for your spiritual growth. Choose to experience His grace instead of being defiled by bitterness.

> **Bitterness starts out as a root, but it grows into a tree.**

Prayerfully consider whether these teachings have touched a nerve. Are you living in bitterness? Have your self-justifying, complaining, and feelings of mistreatment been covers for ongoing bitterness toward God? Has your bitterness spilled over and hurt people you love? If so, ask God for a sweet and humble spirit that releases your bitterness, accepts His grace, and submits to His purposes in your life.

THE LAND OF PROFANE LIVING

Today's Scripture Focus

"See to it . . . that no one is sexually immoral or unholy
like Esau, who sold his birthright for a single meal."
Hebrews 12:15-16

If we don't alter our itinerary, the next stop on our self-destructive journey is the land of profane living. *Profane living* means *godlessness*. Hebrews 12:15-16 says, "See to it . . . that no one is sexually immoral or unholy like Esau." Do you remember Esau? God set apart Abraham to build the nation of Israel. Abraham had a son named Isaac, and Isaac and his wife, Rebecca, had twin boys, Esau and Jacob.

The NKJV says, ". . . looking carefully . . . lest there be any fornicator or profane person like Esau." The Bible does not say that Esau was sexually immoral or an adulterer or a fornicator. Here's what I think it's talking about. The Bible indicates that the greatest form of sin is not unfaithfulness to your spouse or unfaithfulness to your own body but unfaithfulness to God. Look at the following Scriptures.

> " 'You have played the whore with many lovers; and would
> you return to me?' declares the LORD." *Jeremiah 3:1*

> "You adulterous people! Do you know that friendship
> with the world is enmity with God?" *James 4:4*

I think Hebrews 12:15-16 is saying that Esau's immorality was not sexual sin but unfaithfulness to God. That's why the ESV uses "unholy" to describe him. The NIV and NASB say he was "godless." The NKJV uses "profane." The word indicates that Esau was unhallowed, unconcerned with spiritual realities; the things of God meant nothing to Him.

How does the language of sexual impurity in Hebrews 12:15-16 express more graphically the severity of being spiritually unfaithful to God?

The greatest form of sin is not unfaithfulness to your spouse or unfaithfulness to your own body but unfaithfulness to God.

A Tragic Story

Do you remember the account of Jacob and Esau in Genesis 25? Jacob and Esau were twin brothers, but Esau was born first. By birth order Esau had the birthright and the blessing, which represented God's favor. But that didn't mean anything to Esau.

The twins could not have been more different. Jacob loved to stay at home with his mother, cooking and making food in the kitchen. Esau wasn't like that at all. He was a hairy man. He liked to hunt. Esau would be perfect on the cover of *Outdoorsman* magazine. Jacob, on the other hand, would grace the cover of *GQ*. Twins born from the same mom and dad—but so different. But those aren't the differences that matter. What matters is that Jacob loved God. Esau, on the other hand, was never humble and broken, never submissive to God.

Esau came in one day from hunting, and Jacob was in the kitchen. Esau was "Get-out-of-my-way-or-I'll-kill-you" hungry. "Give me whatever you're making there," he demanded. Jacob, seeing his opportunity, said, "Yeah, that smells good, doesn't it?" Then he bargained, "Sell me your birthright for this bowl of stew."

Now what Esau should've said was "Are you crazy? For my birthright I could buy a river of stew!" But he was a profane person. The birthright was a spiritual thing. It was given in a blessing, a prayer from the father. The things of God didn't mean anything to Esau. All he could think of was his immediate discomfort. So instead of valuing his heritage, he responded, "Whatever! Who cares about the birthright? Give me my stew!"

So Jacob thought, *Sweet! That was easy!* And he served up the stew for his brother.

That moment in Scripture is tragic. It shows the heart of a profane person who demonstrated that God meant nothing to him. That happened in a moment, but inwardly it had been happening for a long time. That's the way crises work. They often reveal something that's been happening internally for a long time.

> **Crises often reveal something that's been happening internally for a long time.**

What attitudes were revealed when the following biblical characters faced crises?

Amon, son of David (see 2 Sam. 13:1-22):

Solomon (see 1 Kings 11:1-13):

Jonah (see Jonah 4:1-11):

Judas (see John 12:1-6):

A Warning

When a person travels from the land of bitterness to the land of profane living, behavioral changes that seem to appear suddenly are often simply the public outcome of bitter thoughts and attitudes that have been festering underneath for a long time. It's the kind of stuff that makes you shake your head and wonder, *What would cause a faithful mother of 15 years to turn her back on her husband and her children and run off with some shiftless character? What would cause a businessman with decades of integrity under his belt to suddenly take off with his company's money and end up losing everything? What would cause a pastor who's preached God's Word faithfully for years to . . .*

We've all heard these horror stories. They didn't happen in three minutes. Something had been going on for a while under the surface. It may have started with discouragement that was followed by dislocation, which grew into bitterness, which eventually led to profane living. Inevitably, refusing the trial God has allowed in your life will burst forth in profane living. If you aren't submitting to His work in your life, you won't be able to hold in your anger, bitterness, and resentment. You resent what God has given to other people, and you feel like you've been bypassed. The anger seethes in you, and it's going to come out.

> Inevitably, refusing the trial God has allowed in your life will burst forth in profane living.

Identify ways profane living might be expressed in the life of someone who is resisting God.

If you don't get in a place of submission to God, "be sure your sin will find you out" (Num. 32:23). That private pornography? That secret lust? That deep resentment? It's all going to come out. Maybe it's more subtle. Maybe you've quit going to church or reading your Bible. Whatever the fruit of bitterness is, Jesus wasn't kidding when He said, "Whatever you have said in the dark shall be heard in the light, and what you have whispered in private rooms shall be proclaimed on the housetops" (Luke 12:3).

Consider this a warning. If you continue to refuse God's discipline, bitterness will lead to profane living. And like Esau, a persistent rebel who loses interest in spiritual things is in no position to receive God's blessing.

> **Consider any subtle or not-so-subtle signs that you have entered the land of profane living. If resistance to God's discipline has brought you to a place where your life is out of sync with God's plan, you need to come clean. Talk to God and to a trusted brother or sister in Christ. Make some notes about what you will do, based on what God has shown you during today's study.**

A persistent rebel who loses interest in spiritual things is in no position to receive God's blessing.

Day 5

THE LAND OF DISQUALIFICATION

Today's Scripture Focus

"You know that afterward, when he [Esau] desired
to inherit the blessing, he was rejected, for he found
no chance to repent, though he sought it with tears."
Hebrews 12:17

If you continue refusing the Lord's discipline, you prove that you have never really known the Lord. If you are really God's child, you cannot go this far in resisting God.

Hebrews 12:17 is one of the scariest verses in the Bible. It says that when Esau changed his mind and desired the blessing of the birthright, it was too late. He was rejected. A lot of people think, *I can do what I want. I can think what I want. I'll get right with God when I'm good and ready.* How foolish to think we can put off repentance until it is convenient and then produce a genuine thirst for holiness whenever we want. A right relationship with God isn't something we can create at will. Someone who thinks this way may already dwell in the land of disqualification.

> How foolish to think we can put off repentance until it is convenient.

Getting What We Wanted

We learned in Hebrews 12:15 that God's goal for us during hardship is to obtain His grace. Any step we've ever made spiritually has been only by His grace. We can't refuse and resist and rebel against God's grace, deciding we will come to Him when we are ready. Genesis 6:3 says, "My Spirit shall not strive with man forever" (NKJV). There comes a time when God says, "You think that thing you need to have is so great? You think that's better than I? You think that's going to satisfy you? Then go for it!" As C. S. Lewis often pointed out, if we live our lives refusing to humble ourselves before God and refusing to say, "Thy will be done," God will eventually declare to us, for all eternity, "Thy will be done."[1] The land of disqualification is the off ramp to hell.

Maybe you know people who are living in the land of disqualification. What evidence in their lives shows that they have rejected God to this degree?

Make it a point to pray for these people regularly and to look for opportunities to present the truth about God's desires for them.

If you have rejected God's discipline to the point that you have reached the land of disqualification, pay careful and prayerful attention to the rest of this lesson. Your eternal destiny weighs in the balance.

The land of disqualification is the last stop on this side of eternity. We arrive there when we refuse to accept God's work in our lives. Here God turns us over to the things we think we must have that are more important than He. That's what happened when the Israelites demanded meat in the wilderness.

Read Numbers 11:18-20. What did God do in response to the people's demand?

God gave them so much meat that it ran out of their nostrils and they choked on it. And did it satisfy? Referencing that same scene, the psalmist wrote:

> "[God] gave them their request,
> But sent leanness into their soul." *Psalm 106:15, NKJV*

After we get what we thought we had to have and discover that it doesn't make us happy, we finally conclude that we need God too. Hebrews 12:17 says that afterward Esau wanted to inherit the blessing. It's always afterward. After we have what we had to have, then we realize we want God too. "I want my private pleasure … *and* God." "I want my gluttonous pursuit … *and* God." "I want my material objective … *and* God." "I want both!" That's not going to happen.

Read Psalm 37:4:

> "Delight yourself in the LORD,
> and he will give you the desires of your heart."

After we get what we thought we had to have and discover that it doesn't make us happy, we finally conclude that we need God.

Why are human desires and God's desires sometimes mutually exclusive?

God gives us our desires only when we want what He wants.

God gives us our desires only when we want what He wants. We can't pursue evil and expect Him to work in our lives at the same time. We can't have it both ways.

What Were We Thinking?

One day poor Esau woke up and realized, *What was I thinking? I gave up my birthright for stew? Now that I have what I wanted, I'm going to go get what really matters!* Bad plan. "Afterward, when he desired to inherit the blessing, he was rejected" (Heb. 12:17). *Rejected.* That word, translated *reprobate* in the KJV, is *disqualified* in 1 Corinthians 9:27. It's a horrible term that Paul used to describe his own nightmare—". . . lest after preaching to others I myself should be disqualified."

Paul? Paul was fearful of not making the grade? Right! Paul was aware that his assurance of salvation was not rooted in a prayer he prayed. That's how we *get* saved. But Paul's assurance of salvation was tied up in whether his life gave evidence of a person who was saved. Paul didn't want to be someone who talked about a relationship with God but didn't live it.

I feel the same way. I don't want to tell you all about trials without being faithful to what God is doing in my own life. But you can be assured that I *am* going through hard times and that I *am* seeking to submit fully and embrace what God has allowed in my life. That's what you need to do too. At some point there will be no more time. In the meantime, people are watching your life who will never know you. You can be a living example of holiness for them.

Who are the five persons who are most closely observing your life? Write their first names.

1.

2.

3.

4.

5.

Identify ways you can be their example of the Christian life. How is your current hardship enabling you to do that?

If you're pursuing God with all your heart, you're in a great position to influence other people. But if you enter a hard time and persistently reject His discipline, your heart gets harder and harder, and it becomes more difficult to have any influence for the Kingdom. And if you reach the land of disqualification, it's impossible.

How can you know if it's too late for you, as it was for Esau? If you care, it's not too late. If you flat-out don't care, that should scare you. You should suspect that a root of bitterness growing within you has taken shape into an invasive, poisonous tree that will yield fruit that can never satisfy.

Read Psalm 1, which compares two kinds of lives: those lived God's way and those lived any other way—the righteous and the wicked. What does the life of a wicked person produce?

What are the results of a righteous person's life?

What kind of fruit is being harvested as you face your current trial?

If you aren't producing the fruit of righteousness in your life—if you aren't loving others, going to church, reading the Bible, encouraging others, ministering, sharing the gospel—it's time to check your heart. Has it been poisoned by bitterness?

> If you aren't producing the fruit of righteousness in your life, it's time to check your heart.

A Chance to Repent

Psalm 95:7-8 says:

> "Today, if you hear his voice,
> do not harden your hearts."

Why today? Because if you are in the land of disqualification, you are in a precarious situation, and you don't know if you're going to get tomorrow. You might not have another chance. You don't know whether God is ever going to stir spiritual tenderness in your heart again. The time to respond to God is today—now.

Today's Scripture focus says that after Esau "desired to inherit the blessing, he was rejected, for he found no chance to repent, though he sought it with tears" (Heb 12:17). The NIV inserts, ". . . though he sought the blessing with tears," but the term *blessing* is not in the original Greek. Esau was not seeking the blessing with tears; he was seeking the "chance to repent"—the place of repentance. He tried to repent, but he couldn't. After moving from discouragement to dislocation to bitterness to disqualification, Esau was incapable of being sorry about his past choices. His heart was too hard. He had already eaten the stew. He couldn't sincerely be sorry after he had enjoyed what he wanted. God doesn't play games. Repentance is a serious thing. Repentance is actually changing your mind. It's not easy to repent.

Read these verses:

> "The heart is deceitful above all things,
> and desperately sick;
> who can understand it?" *Jeremiah 17:9*

> "By this we shall know that we are of the truth and reassure
> our heart before him; for whenever our heart condemns us,
> God is greater than our heart, and he knows everything." *1 John 3:19-20*

How can a hardened heart undermine any effort toward repentance?

The time to respond to God is today—now.

It is impossible to arrive at repentance on our own. Repentance requires God's assistance. Second Timothy 2:25 tells us that God is the One who grants repentance. Repentance is a good gift from God. If we have had a hardhearted, bitter attitude toward the difficult season that God has allowed in our lives, we need to ask Him to bring our hearts to repentance. We need to come to a place of genuine, true submission to God about the discipline He has allowed. Remember that He has designed it for your good—to change your conduct and your character.

A man in my church was going through a very painful season. He was a new Christian when a very loved family member unexpectedly died. The funeral was going to be a seriously painful event because the person who died had not known the Lord as personal Savior. My friend was leaning hard on the Lord. When his family gathered, he got up and put in a CD of a song our church sings in worship, "It's All About You." The song makes the point that our relationship with God will not stand if it boils down to God's giving us an easy life on earth and eternal life beyond, without any sorrow or hardship. Life in God is all about fulfilling His purposes.

The grieving man sat there and asked his whole family to listen. Then he said these very profound words for a young believer: "I want God to know that I don't just love Him because I'm going to heaven someday, and I don't just love Him because He does what's good for me. I love God no matter what!"

What has God allowed in your life that you are fighting Him about?

If something came to mind and your relationship with God matters, ask Him to lead you to repentance. Do it today while you can still repent. What do you want to tell Him? Can you say from your heart, "I love You no matter what"?

1. C. S. Lewis, *The Great Divorce* (New York: Touchstone, 1974), 72.

WHY SOME TRIALS NEVER END

This Week's Scripture Focus

"To keep me from becoming conceited because of the surpassing greatness of the revelations, a thorn was given me in the flesh, a messenger of Satan to harass me, to keep me from becoming conceited. Three times I pleaded with the Lord about this, that it should leave me. But he said to me, 'My grace is sufficient for you, for my power is made perfect in weakness.' Therefore I will boast all the more gladly of my weaknesses, so that the power of Christ may rest upon me. For the sake of Christ, then, I am content with weaknesses, insults, hardships, persecutions, and calamities. For when I am weak, then I am strong." *2 Corinthians 12:7-10*

Trials That Last a Lifetime

Some trials are difficult because of their severity; others are difficult because of their length. People who live with chronic pain say that after a while the real hardship is not that it hurts but that they have little hope that it will ever stop hurting. Trials often present themselves as never-ending: *Will this grief ever end? Will I ever stop crying? Will I ever get relief from being overwhelmed each time I think about that person or situation?* You can probably think of experiences that evoked similar reactions, but now you realize that change eventually came and healing gradually occurred. For believers, time often allows us to see yet again that God is in fact working all things together for good (see Rom. 8:28).

Jesus experienced a trial that didn't end on this side of eternity. Instead, it led to His death. Perhaps the darkest moment in that long struggle was the moment close to the end when Jesus recognized that His acceptance of the sins of humankind—yours and mine—had caused God to turn away from Him (see Matt. 27:46). Jesus' crucifixion demonstrates that some trials go all the way. We must let God show us how to live with lengthy trials so that whether they last a lifetime or, by His mercy, just a season, we will get maximum benefit from them.

We have already discovered in this study that Jesus is fully able to understand all we go through because He went through it Himself. We have also learned that we must endure trials just as the Son of God did. All of God's children experience suffering. But we also have God to sustain and help us, and that makes all the difference. This week's lessons focus on what Paul learned from his enduring experience that he called a thorn. God inspired him to give us guidance about how to respond to trials that never seem to end.

Week 5

GROUP EXPERIENCE

As You Gather

1. **What is the longest race you have ever participated in? What was that experience like?**

2. **When you have experienced a hard time in life, what is one word or action someone offered that encouraged you?**

Preparation and Review

1. **Of the five lands you visited last week (discouragement, dislocation, bitterness, profane living, and disqualification), which stop on the tour was most enlightening to you and why?**

2. **Name one way you have made progress in understanding and responding to trials during this study.**

3. **How did last week's assignments affect your desire for and pursuit of holiness?**

DVD Session 5 Viewer Guide

Understanding **Your Thorn (see 2 Cor. 12:7b-8)**

A thorn is an *enduring* source of personal pain allowed by God for our good.

Trials—even thorns—are *allowed* by God.

Five key principles to remember:

1. Omnipotence has its *limits*.

2. The world God made is *good* in its original design, which includes freedom of choice.

3. God could not allow choice and *guarantee* that everyone would choose Him.

4. The effects of sin are visiting themselves _randomly_ on creation.

5. God could _prevent_ the effects of sin; but normally, He allows broken creation to go on as it is.

God inserts Himself _post event_ and promises Himself to us.

Who was the source of Paul's thorn? _Satan_

Satan's goal is to harass and _torment_ us.

When we seek independence from God, we may say:
- I can _handle_ this.
- I can _fix_ this.
- I can _settle_ this.

Living with Your Thorn (see 2 Cor. 12:9-10)

Grace is the package that all blessing comes in.

"Sufficient for you is the grace of _me_."

The grace of Jesus is not fully seen until the _weakness_ is fully experienced.

Two things Paul did that we can do:
1. _Boast_ in your thorn to experience Christ's power.
2. Be _content_ in your thorn to experience Christ's purpose.

How could Paul live contented? For the sake of _Christ_.

Responding to the DVD Teaching

1. **If we followed Paul's approach to handling his thorn, what exactly would we do? What stuck with you from the DVD teaching?**

2. **How do Jesus' words to Paul (see 2 Cor. 12:9) impact your understanding of God's purposes in what you might consider thorns in your life?**

Read week 5 and complete the activities before the next group experience.

UNDERSTANDING YOUR THORN

Today's Scripture Focus

"To keep me from becoming conceited because of the surpassing greatness of the revelations, a thorn was given me in the flesh."

2 Corinthians 12:7

The apostle Paul is famous for his thorn. The word for *thorn* in today's Scripture focus occurs only once in the New Testament. It literally means *a splinter, a stake, a thorn, a small piece of wood embedded in the skin that causes pain.* If you've ever had a thorn in your skin, you know the pain is disproportional to its size.

So what was Paul's thorn? A lot of ink has been spilled trying to answer that question. Many scholars have tried to find hints in the rest of Paul's writing. I had a college professor who thought it was an eye malady because in Galatians 6:11 Paul said, "See with what large letters I am writing to you." Because Paul was writing in big, block letters, my professor assumed he couldn't see very well.

Some people say Paul's thorn was a character flaw that vexed him. Luther thought it was sexual temptation since Paul was single and living in Ephesus, a city known for sexual immorality.

We can all look to God, find comfort and strength, and receive the ministry of the Holy Spirit to respond to our particular thorns.

The fact is that we don't know what Paul's thorn was. The Bible doesn't tell us. If God had wanted us to know, He would have told us. I think it's awesome that we don't know, because otherwise, our understanding of a thorn might be limited to Paul's specific issue. Instead, we know that thorns vary with individual Christians. Like Paul, we can all look to God, find comfort and strength, and receive the ministry of the Holy Spirit to respond to our particular thorns. I think God was immensely wise not to disclose what Paul's thorn was.

Does not knowing Paul's thorn help you or frustrate you? Why?

What Is a Thorn?

Most trials we have talked about in this study come to an end; they don't go on forever. For example, James 1:12 assumes a time will come when the test is over: "Blessed is the man who remains steadfast under trial, for when he has stood the test he will receive the crown of life." When 1 Peter 4:12 tells us, "Do not be surprised at the fiery trial when it comes upon you to test you," it implies that the trial comes for a time and then leaves. The fire goes out. Hebrews 12:11 also indicates that normal trials are just for a season: "For the moment all discipline seems painful rather than pleasant, but later it yields the peaceful fruit of righteousness to those who have been trained by it."

So eventually, a normal trial ends. But the same is not true of a thorn. A thorn is an enduring trial, and not every Christian gets one. A thorn is an enduring source of personal pain allowed by God for our good.

> A thorn is an enduring source of personal pain allowed by God for our good.

Look again at the definition of *thorn* in the previous sentence. Think about past and current trials in your life. In the left column, list trials that you suspected were thorns but proved not to be enduring. In the right column, list trials that were or are potential thorns in your life.

Suspected Thorns　　　　　　**Potential Thorns**

Allowed by God

Today's Scripture focus indicates that Paul's thorn was given to him. Our definition states that a thorn is allowed by God. That phrase *allowed by God* needs some clarification. Honestly, it's a mystery. How could a loving God allow painful, difficult things to happen to His children? This word *allowed* is really important. A thorn isn't directly caused—not by God. Did God give me cancer? Did God cause the heartache and destruction that blew in with Hurricane Katrina in 2005? Did God shake the earth under Port Au Prince, Haiti, in 2010 and cause devastation and death in that already struggling nation? Some people whose faith and theology I greatly respect would say, "Yes, He did." But I don't believe that.

This issue of God's relationship to human suffering is important for every believer to think through. When I walk through deep valleys with people in my church, we frame their trial within the following five biblical borders.

Omnipotence has its limits. When you say God is all-powerful, you have to know what you're talking about. Theologians used to wrestle with questions like "Can God make a rock so big that He can't lift it?" No, He cannot, because no matter how big He made it, He could lift it.

However, omnipotence doesn't mean God can do absolutely anything you can conceive of. There are many things God can't do. God can't make a round square. Though some have tried, God cannot make a married bachelor. Either you're married or you're not.

But I thought God could do anything! God can do anything that can be done. Those other concepts are logical contradictions. God can't contradict or contra-act Himself. File that away for a moment, and we'll come back to it.

The world God made is good. In its original form, as God designed and instituted the world, it was perfect. But it was a very particular kind of world that God wanted to make—He wanted to make a world in which people were free to choose. He could have made a world in which we were all robots. He could have made a world in which we all came to church on Sunday morning at 11:00 a.m. and said, "I worship You. Amen." He could have made it so that we all worshiped Him perfectly. But how much would that mean to Him? If I said to my wife, "Honey, it's Sunday morning at 11:00 a.m. It's time to tell you I love you again. So I love you. I'll see you next week," how meaningful would that be? Not very. My wife doesn't want that, and neither does God. He doesn't want robotic worship. God wants meaningful worship. In order to have meaningful worship, God had to create us with the opportunity to choose. In order to have meaningful obedience, there had to be the possibility of meaningful disobedience.

God made a world in which people were truly free to choose, which means not everyone would choose Him. If God desired mass, robotic worship, He wouldn't have given us the freedom to choose. Instead, He prefers the meaningful worship of those who choose Him. He took a pass on a puppet creation. Because God chose to make a world in which people were free to choose, He could not make a world in which people were free to choose and, at the same time, guarantee that everyone would choose Him.

God wanted to make a world in which people were free to choose.

Given the kind of world God created, the effects of sin randomly visit themselves on creation. It's called sin. In a world in which we were free to choose, we chose to sin. And because of that, creation is broken (see Gen. 3:17-18; Rom. 8:20). The world doesn't work right. People get cancer. People die prematurely. Accidents happen. Marriages fail.

God could prevent the effects of sin. I believe occasionally God intervenes to prevent the effects of sin; but normally, God allows broken creation to go on as it is and horrible events to happen. God doesn't cause those things, but He allows them. But after the event occurs, He promises Himself to the people who face the trial so that we can display the superiority of a life lived in God. We go through the same hardships that people who don't know the Lord go through. Yet our experience is very different.

> **Review the previous principles about God's ongoing relationship with the fallen world. Why do you think it is important to understand that although God allows bad things to happen, He doesn't cause them?**

> **Which one of these five principles helps you better understand why some hard parts of life also turn out to be very long parts of life? Why?**

Some Scriptures state that God caused something bad to happen. Isaiah 45:7 says, "I make peace and create calamity" (NKJV). Yes, God ultimately creates calamity in that He chose to create a world in which people were free to choose. In that sense, God is involved in it. Jonah 1:4,17 says "The Lord sent out a great wind on the sea" (NKJV) and "The Lord had prepared a great fish" (NKJV). God didn't make the fish or the storm from nothing and put it in front of Jonah. God guided and coordinated natural events to accomplish His purposes. But God isn't causally related to suffering in the world that results from sin. God's relationship to causation is this: He created a good world in which people were free to choose. And because humankind has chosen sin, we live in a broken world.

God isn't causally related to suffering in the world that results from sin.

God doesn't have to
prove His sovereignty
by micromanaging
our lives.

On the other hand, our God is not the god of deism, who created the world and then let it spin out of control while He went off to do something else. Our God, who revealed Himself through creation, His Word, and His Son, is thoroughly aware of our suffering and is intimately involved in our lives. He sometimes intervenes to prevent suffering, but most often He uses broken events for our good. God doesn't have to prove His sovereignty by micromanaging our lives. And He doesn't have to directly cause events to make good use of them.

Read Psalm 139 and record examples of God's awareness of and presence in our lives.

Describe your understanding of God's relationship to the thorns in our lives.

Identify an enduring thorn God has allowed in your life. Ask God to guide you to better understand how He wants you to respond to this thorn as you continue this week's lessons.

Day 2

WHO IS THE SOURCE OF PAUL'S THORN?

Today's Scripture Focus

"... a messenger of Satan to harass me,
to keep me from becoming conceited."
2 Corinthians 12:7

The apostle Peter is the target of a lot of jokes. He comes across as an awkward, clumsy guy who didn't know much except fishing. He was so transparently flawed that we find it easy to see our own flaws in him. In spite of the great strength he showed in confessing Jesus as the Son of God (see Matt. 16:16), he was often weak and impulsive. In Luke 22:31 Jesus said to him, "Simon, behold, Satan demanded to have you, that he might sift you like wheat." Did God cause that? No, but just as in the case of Job, God allowed Satan to exercise a certain amount of freedom within boundaries. Three times God allowed Satan to test Peter, and Peter failed the tests. Yet God remained sovereignly and intimately aware of these events without directly intervening. His later work in Peter's life shows that God can do amazing things with sifted wheat!

The Schemer

Who is the source of Paul's thorn? Many people think God gave it to him. But Second Corinthians 12:7, today's Scripture focus, says otherwise. Paul knew the immediate source of his persistent hard spot was Satan. Notice that phrase "messenger of Satan." Paul's thorn was allowed by God but sent by Satan. Satan was the messenger of Paul's thorn.

The text says, "... a messenger of Satan to harass me." The NIV and NASB say, "... to torment me." The NKJV says, "... to buffet me." The term *harass* is a strong word that literally means *to strike with the fist, to box, or to punch*. The immediate results are bumps and bruises—painful but not fatal. It's the same term used in Matthew 26:67 to refer to the blows inflicted on Jesus.

Paul's thorn was allowed by God but sent by Satan.

Read each Scripture and identify the way Satan was harassing someone.

"A demon-oppressed man who was mute was brought to [Jesus]."
Matthew 9:32

"A demon-oppressed man who was blind and mute
was brought to [Jesus]."
Matthew 12:22

"A man came up to [Jesus] and, kneeling before him, said,
'Lord, have mercy on my son, for he is an epileptic and he suffers terribly.
For often he falls into the fire, and often into the water.' "
Matthew 17:14-15

"There was a woman who had had a disabling spirit for eighteen years.
She was bent over and could not fully straighten herself."
Luke 13:11

Scripture consistently teaches that Satan's goal is to harass and torment you. His goal is to paralyze you with fear, to pummel you into painful hopelessness, to make you think all is lost and nothing will change. That's a thorn from Satan. Whatever form they take, thorns are real. They are lasting, tormenting, and satanic. Paul says it's "a thorn ... in the flesh" (2 Cor. 12:7), but that doesn't mean it has to be physical. A thorn is something that torments your humanity. It could be:

• in your mind—a persistent doubt;

• in your emotions—a grief that won't fade;

• in your will—a stubborn, persistent point of moral or spiritual failure.

No matter where Satan attacks, his goal is to harass and torment you.

No matter where Satan attacks, his goal is to harass and torment you.

Think about an enduring thorn you are experiencing. Identify whether it is—

☐ **physical;**   ☐ **mental;**   ☐ **emotional;**   ☐ **moral;**   ☐ **spiritual.**

For Your Good

Recall our definition of *trial:* a painful circumstance allowed by God to change our conduct and our character. We have seen that God allows trials for our good. A thorn is no different. You don't have to be able to see the good that's coming; you don't have to be able to conceive of it; it's not up to you to figure it out. It's God's job to figure that out. You may never be able to figure it out, but God has promised that it's His goal to use your thorn for good. He has promised, "For those who love God all things work together for good, for those who are called according to his purpose" (Rom. 8:28).

Read Job 1:12:

> "The LORD said to Satan, 'Behold, all that he has is in your hand.
> Only against him do not stretch out your hand.' "

What restriction did God place on Satan's first testing of Job?

Read Job 2:6:

> "The LORD said to Satan, 'Behold, he is in your hand; only spare his life.' "

What restriction did God place on Satan's second testing of Job?

Read Job 42:1-6:

> "Job answered the LORD and said:
> 'I know that you can do all things,
> and that no purpose of yours can be thwarted.
> "Who is this that hides counsel without knowledge?"
> Therefore I have uttered what I did not understand,
> things too wonderful for me, which I did not know.
> "Hear, and I will speak;
> I will question you, and you make it known to me."
> I had heard of you by the hearing of the ear,
> but now my eye sees you;
> therefore I despise myself,
> and repent in dust and ashes.' "

From these words, what do you think was the purpose of Job's thorn?

God has promised that it's His goal to use your thorn for good.

The Pride Factor

Paul could relate. He described the positive purpose of his thorn this way: "...to keep me from becoming conceited" (2 Cor. 12:7). Other translations say, "...lest I be exalted" (NKJV) or "...so that I would not feel too proud" (CEV). You might think, *Paul's problem may have been pride, but that's certainly not my problem.* Careful. More than ego or an inflated sense of self-importance, a much more insidious pride problem could be your sense of independence: *I can handle this. I can fix this. I can do this.*

That's where the thorn's going—to keep you from coming to the place in life where you think you have everything under control.

That's where the thorn's going—to keep you from coming to the place in life where you think you have everything under control: *I have it going on! There's really not a whole lot that could tank my boat. I've learned how to navigate through life. Nothing can really make me go under at this point.* That's the pride factor Paul is referring to. He is applying his own words from 1 Corinthians 10:12: "Let anyone who thinks that he stands take heed lest he fall."

I was talking on the phone to a man I had known and loved for years. I could barely hear his voice through his weeping. Through his sobs he said, "Today is the best day of my life. I finally see it. I can't do this myself. I'm not smart enough. I'm not dedicated enough. I'm not even godly enough." Only as he stared with stark finality down the throat of his total inability to accomplish what was in front of him did he come to the place where he could say, "I get it. It's not about me." That's the good God wants to bring about through your thorn.

What have you learned that you can't do from a trial or a thorn?

How did your trial or thorn teach you that you can't do it?

Several years ago I was greeting people after a service when a woman approached me, clearly upset, to tell me something one of my staff members had said—something I'm sure he didn't say. I tried to help, but I couldn't, and she didn't listen very well. It was a very painful conversation. I had another pastor pray with her, and I thought that was the end of it until Wednesday, when I received a very hurtful letter from her. After rehearsing the situation from her perspective, she closed with "You're nothing but a donkey—a big donkey."

That just wasn't a great day, and I've got to admit I was pretty upset about it. Normally, I would have dismissed it; but I was overtired from dealing with other hard issues. For two days I walked around thinking, *I'm nothing but a donkey—a big donkey*. It got lodged in my spirit, and I couldn't get rid of it.

On Friday I was having lunch with the pastor of Moody Church, Erwin Lutzer, a mentor I respect. I didn't tell him anything about the donkey comment because I didn't have it figured out myself. At the end of lunch, Dr. Lutzer walked me back to my car and said, "You know, James, God is really using your life."

I said, "Thanks." It meant a lot to me for him to say that.

Then he said, "So you need to stay humble." Well, that's a good word. Who doesn't need to hear that? So I thanked him for that.

And then right out of the blue he said, ". . . because you know what they say about the donkey, don't you?"

I said, "Uh, no. What do they say?"

This is awesome. He said, "Even the donkey knew the palm branches and the blankets were for the Person on his back and not for him."

Well, I got out of there fast—into my car and on the freeway. I'm not embarrassed to tell you I shed a few tears on the way home as I had this great time with the Lord: "That's it! I'm a donkey! It doesn't matter about me. It doesn't matter what people say. It doesn't matter what people think about me, because it's not about me! It's about You, Lord! Everything I do—it's for You! I have to keep reminding myself. Even the donkey knows that!"

We can use thorns as occasions to blame God or to praise God. Satan's purpose is always trumped by God's purposes, which are always higher and for our good.

We can use thorns as occasions to blame God or to praise God.

Identify an occasion in your life when something that first struck you as offensive, hurtful, and thornlike turned out to give you a startling, humbling, fresh understanding of God.

Thank God that He loves you enough to let your feelings get hurt in order to remind you that you can't do it and are completely dependent on Him.

Day 3
LIVING WITH YOUR THORN

Today's Scripture Focus
"Three times I pleaded with the Lord about this,
that it should leave me. But he said to me, 'My grace is sufficient
for you, for my power is made perfect in weakness.' "
2 Corinthians 12:8-9

Why was God allowing this thorn in Paul's life? Paul's spiritual résumé was awesome. But the Corinthians constantly questioned him, attacking his apostleship, his motives, his speaking style, everything. In 2 Corinthians Paul was defending his apostleship when he said:

"I must go on boasting. Though there is nothing to be gained by it, I will go on to visions and revelations of the Lord. I know a man in Christ who fourteen years ago was caught up to the third heaven—whether in the body or out of the body I do not know, God knows. And I know that this man was caught up into paradise—whether in the body or out of the body I do not know, God knows—and he heard things that cannot be told, which man may not utter." *2 Corinthians 12:1-4*

The thorn came to keep Paul from being conceited.

Paul said he couldn't even tell what he heard. It was so awesome that it would make your head explode. That's when the thorn came to keep Paul from being conceited (v. 7). "Lest I be exalted above measure" is the NKJV translation.

Why do you think something as drastic as a thorn was required to fulfill God's purposes in Paul's life?

Pleading with God
Paul didn't take his thorn lying down. He wrote, "Three times I pleaded with the Lord about this, that it should leave me" (2 Cor. 12:8). If you know anything about prayer, this wasn't like praying at breakfast, lunch, and bedtime. Paul was referring to three extended periods of prayer that went something like this: "I prayed and asked God to take the thorn away, but He didn't. So I went along as far as I could, and then I started praying again, 'God, I can't take this anymore!

I'm losing it! You've got to take this away from me.' But God didn't. So I went on for another season, enduring and persevering. But then I couldn't take it anymore, so I came back a third time and cried, 'God! You've got to take this out of my life! It's too much for me!' "

And finally, the third time Paul got an answer. Does that remind you of Jesus in the garden of Gethsemane? In Matthew 26:39 Jesus prayed to His Father, "Let this cup pass from Me" (NKJV). In verse 42 He repeated, "If this cup cannot pass away from Me unless I drink it, Your will be done" (NKJV). Then in verse 44 we are told that He prayed a third time, "saying the same words" (NKJV). I love that model of submission. Jesus got it done in three hours, but none of us can fast-track that process.

Jesus submitted because God apparently told Him the cup wasn't leaving. In the garden when the soldiers came to arrest Jesus, Peter pulled out his sword and fought back, cutting off the ear of the high priest's servant. After Jesus healed the servant's ear, He turned to Peter and said, "Shall I not drink the cup that the Father has given me?" (John 18:11). Jesus was saying, "What else am I going to do? When it comes right down to it, everything I say I believe is on the line right now. Of course I'm going to drink the cup! There is no other choice. I'm going to keep going."

> **"Of course I'm going to drink the cup!"**

Think about a thorn you are experiencing or someone you know is experiencing. How does each metaphor help you understand lasting hardship in life?

Thorn:

Cup:

If you live with a thorn, would you say you are drinking the cup of suffering like Jesus or fighting like Peter?

My Grace Is Sufficient

Notice the answer Paul received to his requests for deliverance from his thorn: "He [Jesus] said to me, 'My grace is sufficient for you, for my power is made perfect in weakness' " (2 Cor. 12:9). "He said to me" is in the perfect tense. It means Jesus said it, and that settled it. Paul must have been hanging on to these words: "I have this. Jesus said it. It's done."

Jesus said to Paul, "My grace is sufficient. If you're going to get through your thorn, you've got to have My grace." Your thorn will crush you without God's grace. Without grace you will become bitter in a flash.

God's grace is the package that all blessing comes in. Scripture repeatedly calls it the grace of Christ (see Rom. 16:20,24; Gal. 6:18; Phil. 4:23; 1 Thess. 5:28; 2 Thess. 3:18; Philem. 25). That grace is sufficient for everything we need in the Christian life.

The familiar definition of *grace* is *unmerited favor*, but it's so much more than that. Grace is the capacity to do anything spiritually profitable. You can't pray without grace. You can't understand the Bible without grace. You can't choose right over wrong without grace. And you can't get through this thorn without grace. That's why Jesus said to Paul, "My grace is sufficient for you." Those same words are meant for us. Stick with the grace of Jesus Christ all the way to eternity.

Notice the word *sufficient* in 2 Corinthians 12:9. In Greek the words come in this order: "Sufficient for you is the grace of Me." Jesus was saying, "I am the grace."

God doesn't dispense strength and encouragement the way a druggist fills a prescription: "Take two of these and call Me in the morning." He *is* the grace. He *is* the strength. His presence is power! No matter what we need, Jesus is the answer. "Sufficient for you is the grace of Me." He is the grace! He doesn't give it and then move on, like Santa dropping off presents. He comes to stay in an intimate relationship with you: "I am with you always" (Matt. 28:20).

> God's grace is the package that all blessing comes in.

In what ways has Jesus' grace been sufficient for you while you were suffering from a thorn?

Jesus continued speaking to Paul: "My grace is sufficient for you, for my power is made perfect in weakness" (2 Cor. 12:9). *Perfect* in this verse means *fulfilled, accomplished, completed, finished*. It's the same word Jesus spoke as His final utterance on the cross: "It is finished" (John 19:30). The same power Jesus displayed in defeating sin is available to help you endure your thorn.

Second Corinthians 12:9 also says Jesus' strength is made perfect or complete in your weakness. You never really get Jesus' grace unless you realize your need for it. And even that realization is grace. We don't fully see Jesus' grace until we fully experience weakness.

> **Weaknesses are hard for us to admit. We often think our relationships depend on the strengths we bring to them. Yet in our relationship with Jesus, any strength we bring has little value. Talk to Jesus and admit your weakness in dealing with your thorn. Ask Him to give you His grace and His strength as you admit your dependence on Him. Praise Him because His grace is sufficient for you.**

We don't fully see Jesus' grace until we fully experience weakness.

BOASTING IN WEAKNESS

Today's Scripture Focus

"I will boast all the more gladly of my weaknesses,
so that the power of Christ may rest upon me."
2 Corinthians 12:9

If you aren't delivered during your lifetime, your thorn will end when you die.

I don't know where Paul's life ended up. In all likelihood, Paul kept struggling with his thorn until the day he died. Some thorns seem to go on forever, but they won't. If you aren't delivered during your lifetime, your thorn will end when you die. So if you have a persistent thorn, how do you live with it? Paul identified two things you can do. We will look at one today and another tomorrow.

Boast in Your Thorn

In today's Scripture focus Paul said he would boast in his thorn: "I will boast all the more gladly of my weaknesses" (2 Cor. 12:9). To boast about your thorn means to brag about it, to glory in it. You might respond, "James, my marriage is crumbling. My illness is chronic. My grief is crushing me. My thorn is consuming. And you want me to brag about it?" What does God want you to do? Paul said to boast gladly.

Read Jeremiah 9:23-24:

"Thus says the LORD:
'Let not the wise man boast in his wisdom,
let not the mighty man boast in his might,
let not the rich man boast in his riches,
but let him who boasts boast in this,
that he understands and knows me,
that I am the LORD who practices steadfast love,
justice, and righteousness in the earth.
For in these things I delight,
declares the LORD.' "

What do these verses say we are to boast about?

☐ **Strength** ☐ **Knowing God** ☐ **Wisdom** ☐ **Wealth**

I remember standing in a worship service not long ago reflecting on the depth God had brought to my prayer life and my time in His Word, as well as the testimony I had to share about the ways my trials had altered me. The thought crossed my mind, *I'm not glad this trial happened, but I am grateful for the ways God has used it to grow me.* Then I remember feeling a little quiver of anxiety. *I don't ever want to go back to the person I was before I went through this trial.* That gave me insight into what it means to boast gladly in my weakness.

What traits, habits, and thought patterns have been reshaped or removed by trials you have experienced?

The Power of Christ

Paul said he would boast about his weakness "so that the power of Christ may rest" on him (2 Cor. 12:9). Boasting in weakness brings spiritual power because it recognizes your inadequacy and exalts Jesus' sufficiency. Here are some practical ways you can boast about your thorn.

Count your blessings. Counting your blessings is boasting in your thorn. Recounting your blessings will necessitate sharing your hard circumstances along with ways God has shown Himself faithful. You are boasting when you say, "God allowed this thorn in my life, but look at all the good that has come from it!"

Elevate your prayer life. Let your thorn drive you to communicate with focus, with fervency, and with frequency in God's presence. There was a time in my life, I am ashamed to say, when I had been a pastor for more than a decade but didn't know what it meant to get on my face before God. I can't say that anymore. I don't want to go back there. Yes, it was easier; but it was emptier! I don't want to be that person anymore. I'm thankful that God has taught me how to pray.

Lengthen and deepen your time in God's Word. No more little quiet times. No more reading a little story from *The Daily Crouton* and getting a little snippet to think about for the next three minutes. Deepen your time in God's Word. Go deeply into a passage of Scripture and let it become your treasure:

"Oh how I love your law!
It is my meditation all the day." *Psalm 119:97*

> Boasting in weakness brings spiritual power because it recognizes your inadequacy and exalts Jesus' sufficiency.

Focus on your
dependence on
God and what you
are learning.

Tell your story to people. You boast in your weakness when you tell people what God is doing through your trial. You don't have to dwell on the gruesome details; focus on your dependence on God and what you are learning. Don't hide the humor, irony, and unexpected insights you've stumbled over along the way. And resist the temptation to make the problem bigger or yourself wiser in the telling.

Improve your storytelling by listening to others. Note how they report their experiences as you track your own responses. From one person you will discover that it's possible to turn a story into an epic and leave everyone asleep. Someone else will help you see that some details aid understanding, while others just make listeners sick. John the Baptist had a great guiding principle: "He [Jesus] must increase, but I must decrease" (John 3:30). Let those words shape the telling of your story. Your aim is to show how much Christ has increased in your life—how much He has done for you and how faithful He has been.

Focus on the prize. Keep reminding yourself where this is all going. We are locked in time. From our perspective, God's plan seems to be working itself out so slowly, but eternity is racing toward us. So "set your minds on things that are above, not on things that are on earth. For you have died, and your life is hidden with Christ in God" (Col. 3:2-3). Your thorn will not go with you when you cross the finish line!

Paul always talked about the Day of the Lord: "I know whom I have believed and am persuaded that He is able to keep what I have committed to Him until the Day" (2 Tim. 1:12, NKJV). "Henceforth there is laid up for me the crown of righteousness, which the Lord, the righteous judge, will award to me on that Day" (2 Tim. 4:8). Paul couldn't wait for the time when his trials would be over, and he would be with Jesus. Focus on the prize.

> **If you are living with a thorn, identify specific ways you are ready to boast about your weaknesses and magnify Jesus' power. How is God blessing you and teaching you through this difficult season of life?**

When you boast about your weaknesses in living with your thorn, you acknowledge that all of your strength comes from Christ. Boast gladly.

Day 5
CONTENTMENT IN TRIALS

Today's Scripture Focus

"For the sake of Christ, then, I am content with weaknesses,
insults, hardships, persecutions, and calamities.
For when I am weak, then I am strong."
2 Corinthians 12:10

In 2 Corinthians 12:9-10 Paul identified two things we can do to live with a thorn. Yesterday we examined boasting about the thorn. In today's Scripture focus Paul adds, "For the sake of Christ, then, I am content with weaknesses" (v. 10). The second admonition for living with a thorn is to be content with weaknesses in order to experience Christ's strength.

> Be content with weaknesses in order to experience Christ's strength.

Content with the Thorn

Being content with weaknesses doesn't mean you like the thorn, that you want it, or that you enjoy it. But you accept it. You submit to it. You embrace it. By God's grace you rest in it. You say, "I'm not putting my life on hold. I'm not counting the seconds until the thorn is removed. I'm not just getting by and refusing to enjoy anything else. With God's help and for Jesus' sake, I'm living my life with the thorn."

Thorns that are physical. The NKJV translates *weaknesses* in 2 Corinthians 12:10 as "infirmities," meaning "I am content with thorns that are physical trials." But Paul went beyond physical weaknesses.

Thorns that are insults. Insults or "reproaches" (NKJV) are relational thorns, the intentional and unintentional barbs that others inflict on us.

Thorns that are hardships. These are lasting trials dealing with financial and material matters. The KJV uses "necessities" for these material thorns—bankruptcy, foreclosure, and poverty.

Thorns that are persecutions. These personal attacks are spiritual thorns—suffering for the name of Christ.

Thorns that are calamities. *Calamity* literally means *distress*. These are emotional thorns—fear, anxiety, and personal disasters.

If you are enduring a thorn, classify it by checking the applicable type.

☐ **Physical** ☐ **Insult** ☐ **Hardship** ☐ **Persecution** ☐ **Calamity**

Read Philippians 4:10-13 and 1 Timothy 6:6-8. Paul said he had learned contentment. Based on your study this week, how do you think a believer learns contentment?

For the Sake of Christ

How could Paul be content when experiencing insults, hardships, persecutions, and calamities? His answer is right at the beginning of 2 Corinthians 12:10: "For the sake of Christ." Paul could be content because he loved Christ so much. Because it's all about Him. Because He is the purpose of our existence. Because He is the reason we are here. Because we live for His glory and His fame. Because He's in control of the details, and if He has allowed this thorn to come into your life, He also promises, "My grace is sufficient for you, for my power is made perfect in weakness" (2 Cor. 12:9).

If He has allowed this thorn to come into your life, He also promises, "My grace is sufficient for you."

Read 2 Corinthians 5:14-15:

"The love of Christ controls us, because we have concluded this:
that one has died for all, therefore all have died; and he died for all,
that those who live might no longer live for themselves
but for him who for their sake died and was raised."

How does the love of Christ compel you to live with your thorn?

What has your thorn taught you to deny in yourself and to embrace for the sake of Christ?

What strength has come to your life by relying on Jesus as you endure your thorn?

I don't understand it all. I just know God promises, "For those who love God all things work together for good" (Rom. 8:28). And when I rest in His strength, even though I am weak, I am strong.

Think about trials in your life and a thorn you may be living with. Based on your study this week, explain why you think God has allowed these hurts in your life.

> When I rest in His strength, even though I am weak, I am strong.

COME FORTH AS GOLD

This Week's Scripture Focus

"He knows the way that I take;
  when he has tried me, I shall come out as gold."
Job 23:10

God's Refining Process

We've saved the best part for last. When you think of trials and suffering, the first person who springs to mind is probably Job. You might call him the poster boy for suffering. God allowed this good man to be tested beyond what most of us can imagine. He lost his sons, his daughters, his livestock, and his servants. Later he even lost his health and was covered with boils from head to foot. Although Job didn't understand why God was allowing him to suffer, he remained faithful to God, holding on to the conviction that He could be trusted. Job accurately summed up God's refining process when he said:

"He knows the way that I take;
when he has tried me, I shall come out as gold." *Job 23:10*

This picture of the refining process vividly depicts the concept of God's purposes behind trials. Allow me to give you a lesson in Gold 101. To be refined, gold must first be melted. When gold ore comes out of the ground, it is mixed with other metals and impurities. So it is placed in furnaces and heated to 1,010 degrees Celsius, the temperature that melts gold.

The second refiner's step is binding. Once the gold is molten, it is mixed with a special flux to make it more fluid and to bind the impurities together. Then, when the gold is poured into a mold, the impurities, called slag, rise to the top.

Finally, the gold is separated. After it has cooled, the slag is broken off. Then the steps are repeated, sometimes multiple times for greater purity. This process hasn't changed in thousands of years. Technology hasn't improved it. God has given us a lasting illustration of His methods of refining us.

That's what Job had in mind when he said, "When he has tried me, I shall come out as gold." Although he questioned the reason behind God's methods, He never rebelled against God. Your trial is refining you. Do you feel the heat? Can you see the slag rising to the surface? Slag is what makes you restless and miserable and fearful and selfish. Is God drawing the impurities in your life to the surface so that you can come out of this trial as gold?

Some people go into the furnace of affliction and get burned; others go in and get purified. If you submit to the Lord, as painful as the crisis may be, it will refine you and make you better. If you resist what God is doing, the furnace will only burn. If this trial is making your faith purer and stronger and you're not bitter toward the Lord and you're learning to love and trust Him more, you are coming out as gold.

Week 6

GROUP EXPERIENCE

As You Gather

1. If we met again a year from now to review what we learned from this study, what do you think would still be vivid in your mind? Why?

2. Identify someone who is an outstanding example of grace in a trial. What have you learned from that person?

Preparation and Review

1. What have you learned about thorns this week? In what way are thorns different from other trials?

2. What is the source of thorns? Why does God allow them in our lives?

3. What are practices we can apply to live with thorns?

DVD Session 6 Viewer Guide

Every trial we face is allowed by God for our _ultimate_ good.

1. Trials are not _consequences_ (see 1 Pet. 4:14-15).

2. *Good* means all we _need_, not all we want (see Jas. 1:4).

3. _ultimate_, not immediate (see Heb. 12:11)

4. _allowed_, not caused (see 2 Cor. 12:7b-8)

Trials need not steal our _joy_.

1. Because they bring to us the _power_ of God (see 2 Cor. 12:9)

2. Because they _prove_ we are God's children (see Heb. 12:5-8)

3. Because they increase our _endurance_ (see Jas. 1:2-3)

4. Because they _Build_ our intimacy with Jesus (see 1 Pet. 4:13)

God is never more _present_ than when His children are suffering.

1. He is an experienced _sufferer_, fellowshipping with us (see 1 Pet. 4:14).

2. He is an attentive _Counselor_, listening to us (see Jas. 1:5).

3. He is a loving _father_, chastening us (see Heb. 12:6-9).

4. He is a faithful _friend_, sustaining us (see 2 Cor. 12:9).

Until I embrace my trial in unwavering _Submission_ to God, I will not reap the good.

1. The good won't come until I _embrace_ the trial (see 2 Cor. 12:10).

2. I can't embrace my trial without _Submission_ to God (see Heb. 12:9-11).

3. I can maintain my submission only through _Believing prayer_ (see Jas. 1:6-8).

4. I will not reap the good unless I _persevere_ (see 1 Pet. 4:19).

Responding to the DVD Teaching

1. **Which one of the main points from the DVD teaching would you most like to discuss at greater length? Why?**

2. **As we come to the final week of this study, how would you describe your outlook for future trials?**

Read week 6 and complete the activities to conclude your study of _When Life Is Hard_.

If you missed this session, you can download the DVD teaching from
www.lifeway.com/downloads.

Day 1
THE WAY TO ULTIMATE GOOD

Today's Scripture Focus
"He knows the way that I take;
when he has tried me, I shall come out as gold."
Job 23:10

Each day this week we will tour all four main Bible passages we have explored during this study, focusing on a central idea or principle each day. Today's principle is this:

Every trial you face is allowed by God for your ultimate good.

This truth is the rock your feet need to be on when the waves of satanic lies threaten to sweep you under, the anchor you can hold on to in the storm, the wind that fills your sails of hope, and the light that guides your ship of faith safely into the harbor.

Job's world crumbled when Satan was allowed to take away his family and possessions. But notice what Job did: "Job arose and tore his robe and shaved his head and fell on the ground and worshiped. And he said, 'Naked I came from my mother's womb, and naked shall I return. The Lord gave, and the Lord has taken away; blessed be the name of the Lord.' In all this Job did not sin or charge God with wrong" (Job 1:20-22). Instead of turning against God, Job worshiped Him.

In today's Scripture focus Job expressed confidence that God was aware of his pain: "He knows the way that I take" (Job 23:10). Job kept his faith in God's goodness, and this rock was the solid foundation on which he took his stand. In the end Job knew he would come out as gold.

> Instead of turning against God, Job worshiped Him.

Where Did This Pain Come From?
When you find yourself in a hard circumstance, always ask, *Am I suffering in a trial, or is my pain a consequence of something I've done?* To answer that question, you have to identify the source of that hard thing in your life, because your

responsibility in the matter depends on the source of your hardship. If your difficulty is waking you up to the reality of your bad choices, it's a consequence. A painful consequence is something you reap when you plant a seed full of sin—something harmful you've done, harsh words you've spoken, places you've gone, wrong priorities you've pursued, commitments you've neglected, or selfish choices you've made. If you are harvesting heartache today from a sin you've previously planted, it's time to humbly repent of your actions.

Many believers are experiencing very painful consequences of sin in their lives. They may call those consequences trials, but "do not be deceived," Galatians 6:7 says. "God is not mocked, for whatever one sows, that will he also reap."

If, on the other hand, your hardship is something God has allowed to train your conduct or your character, you are in a trial. An example is persecution for the sake of Christ. First Peter 4:14 says, "If you are insulted for the name of Christ, you are blessed, because the Spirit of glory and of God rests upon you." Or perhaps God has allowed illness or a difficult relationship to disrupt your life. Although you did nothing to cause these trials, God wants to teach you through them as you submit to His loving discipline.

> **Identify the following situations as trials (T) or consequences (C).**
>
> **"My marriage is in trouble after many years of neglect."**   ☐ **T** ☐ **C**
>
> **"My husband lost his job because the car industry is suffering."** ☐ **T** ☐ **C**
>
> **"My husband lost his job because he stole things from work."**   ☐ **T** ☐ **C**
>
> **"My son has a serious illness and is in the hospital."**   ☐ **T** ☐ **C**

First Peter 4 continues with a warning about the consequences of sin: "Let none of you suffer as a murderer or a thief or an evildoer or as a meddler" (v. 15).

- *Murderer* describes someone with a hateful action or thought—someone who disrespects life.

- *Thief* describes someone who loses his or her job for stealing time, someone who loses his or her marriage for stealing selfish interests, or someone who loses his or her friend by stealing too much attention. All of these actions involve taking what belongs to someone else.

- *Evildoer* is a general term for someone who participates in sinful activity.

A painful consequence is something you reap when you plant a seed full of sin.

- *Meddler* describes someone who, as the NLT puts it, is "prying into other people's affairs."

If one of these conditions is causing your hardship, you are suffering a consequence, not a trial. Although we are forgiven the penalty of sin, we must still suffer the harvest of consequences when we sin. Wrong actions have wrong consequences, even for Christians.

If you are suffering consequences, repent now. Turn around and run back to God.

> **We have a devious habit of looking for someone else to blame. When identifying our difficulties as trials or consequences, start with, *What's my responsibility here? Am I contributing to my own hardship by thoughtless choices or wrong actions?* Make these questions a prayer. Ask God to point out any sinful ways that have contributed to your trial. Then listen to what He says.**

Needs Versus Wants

Every trial we face is allowed by God for our ultimate good. That means good things are coming from our trials. God has promised us, "I know the plans I have for you, declares the LORD, plans for welfare and not for evil, to give you a future and a hope" (Jer. 29:11).

James 1:2-4 tells us that during trials God gives us what we need: "Count it all joy ... when you meet trials of various kinds. ... And let steadfastness have its full effect, *that you may be perfect and complete, lacking in nothing"* (italics added). Trials often show up when we're not getting what we want. God demonstrates His wisdom and His love for us by allowing into our lives what we need.

God demonstrates His wisdom and His love for us by allowing into our lives what we need.

One of the great pains in life is that things are not always the way we want them to be. But God makes sure we have everything we need. When Scripture says God is working everything out for our ultimate good (see Rom. 8:28), that doesn't mean we're going to have everything we want. As James 1:4 says, our steadfastness (our endurance) leads to our being "perfect," "complete," and "lacking in nothing." What great terms!

- *Perfect*—we will have all the character we need to honor God.

- *Complete*—we will have all of the relationships we need to nourish and sustain us.

• *Lacking in nothing*—we will miss nothing that would give us 100 percent satisfaction in God.

If we are perfect and complete, lacking in nothing, we have everything we need to do everything God wants us to do. We can show the world the superiority of a life lived in God.

Every trial we face is allowed by God for our ultimate good. That good includes our ability to discern the difference between needs and wants. Today if we endure, God promises to give us what we need. Tomorrow, in heaven, God promises to give us everything we could ever want and more.

For now let's be thankful and content. We have everything we need to do everything God wants us to do.

Record something you want during your current trial.

Record what you need during your trial.

How is God giving you what you need to gain all He wants you to get from this experience?

How do you need to submit to God's work to make you perfect, complete, and lacking in nothing?

Tomorrow, in heaven, God promises to give us everything we could ever want and more.

It Takes Time

God is working our trials for our ultimate good, but it takes time. We aren't the first Christians who have ever lived. Walking by faith, not by sight, has been going on for generations. The pages of Scripture and church history are filled with people who relied on the truths we've examined in this study to prove God faithful in their generation. Our challenge is to do the same in our trials. Our faithful predecessors would tell us that the trial we face today will turn out to be for our ultimate good. It may not seem so today, but it really will.

I love the honesty of Hebrews 12:11: "For the moment all discipline seems painful rather than pleasant." Discipline seems painful because it is, but "later it yields the peaceful fruit of righteousness." If you're patient, there's fruit coming, as a farmer harvests a crop long after he planted the seed.

Do you already see the peaceful fruit of righteousness growing in your life as a result of a trial? ☐ **Yes** ☐ **No**

Do you see yourself changed by God's training during your trial? ☐ **Yes** ☐ **No**

> **Any growth during a trial is conditioned on our cooperating with what God is doing.**

Any growth during a trial is conditioned on our cooperating with what God is doing. And often, the good that God is bringing to our lives can be seen only through the perspective of time. The purpose of this trial is for our transformation, so that we can stand in that long line of generations of Christians—"so great a cloud of witnesses" (Heb. 12:1)—who are shouting, "Keep going! Good is coming! It will all be worth it. Don't give up! Look to Jesus!"

Because God's promise of ongoing training is for life, the choices and decisions you make during a trial need to be made with eternity in mind, not your momentary discomfort. In what specific ways are you remaining under God's discipline for your ultimate benefit?

Turning It Around for Good

In spite of what you may have heard, God allows bad things to happen to good people. He doesn't cause them, but He doesn't prevent them either. God created us with free will. In the circumstances of life, He rarely steps in to alter the fact that the effects of sin are randomly visiting themselves on creation. So God lets trials happen to Christians just as He lets them happen to pagans. Why? So that we can demonstrate the superiority of a life lived in God. The majority of the world is choosing not to worship God; but a few of us, by God's grace, are depending on God's promised resources to get us through our trials.

God did not cause the horrible events in your life, but you need to embrace the fact that He allowed them. God could not make a world in which we are free and at the same time guarantee that everyone would choose Him. So the world is broken, and bad things happen. But God promises that He will work for good in the lives of those who love Him (see Rom. 8:28). He will bring us through the fire, and we will come out as gold.

God allowed Paul to suffer a "thorn ... in the flesh, a messenger of Satan to harass me, to keep me from becoming conceited" (2 Cor. 12:7). Paul understood that God allowed this pain in his life for a reason. God allowed a demon to harass, or buffet (NKJV) Paul. The word *buffet* means *to strike with a fist or beat*. But God permitted it with a good purpose: to keep the apostle from being conceited.

God is always sovereign. He is so much in control that even when Satan tries to ruin our lives, God takes the weapon Satan wants to use to destroy us and turns it into a good thing. God says, "If you will lean hard on Me in the midst of this difficult time, I'll take that thorn and make it work for your good."

We all have something God has allowed into our lives that Satan meant for our destruction but that God has turned around to help us grow and change. God, help us choose again today to trust You with it.

> **Have you identified a thorn in your life? If nothing comes to mind, ask yourself whether you're angry in, disappointed in, or resentful toward God about something. That would be a good place to look for a thorn. Once you've located the thorn (if you have one), it's time to decide what you are going to do about it. Are you ready to acknowledge that God has allowed this thorn for your ultimate good? Are you ready to trust Him with the outcome? Spend time in prayer submitting your thorn to God's purposes for your life.**

God promises that He will work for good in the lives of those who love Him.

Day 2

KEEP THE JOY

Today's Scripture Focus
"He knows the way that I take;
when he has tried me, I shall come out as gold."
Job 23:10

I was not a great youth pastor. One reason I was so lame was that I hate theme parks. Even more than theme parks, I hate roller coasters. I could take you to places all around North America where kids talked me into riding on crazy, convoluted, death-defying, twisting roller coasters. I've left more vomit on more rides and riders than I can count. Needless to say, I'll never ride a roller coaster *ever* again!

But I have a confession to make: even though I don't ride roller coasters anymore, sometimes I make the foolish choice to get on an emotional roller coaster. It used to be that on any given day I was doing well, and then something bad happened, and I went into the tank. Then there was good news—but wait. Then there was bad news—no, wait, I'm OK again. I rode emotional highs, lows, and corkscrews. That's an awful way to live. I've come to the place now where I acknowledge that trials need not steal my joy.

If you've lost your joy, it doesn't have to be that way. You can get off the roller coaster by focusing on the presence and power of God in any circumstance. No trial needs to steal your joy. Joy that never fades is one way you come out of your trial as gold. So this is our principle for today:

Your trial doesn't need to steal your joy.

Strength in Weakness

I'm writing this on an awful day. Some very heavy things have hit Kathy and me to knock us off balance. But somewhere in the middle of that storm, God's voice is telling me that He provides sufficient grace for this trial, and when I am weak, He is always very strong. If anything in this study is powerful, it is from my weakness.

> Joy that never fades is one way you come out of your trial as gold.

"I will boast all the more gladly of my weaknesses, so that the power of Christ may rest upon me. ... For when I am weak, then I am strong" (2 Cor. 12:9-10). The hard times and the unhealthy times and the hurting times reveal my weaknesses. But it's also during those times that God shows up and proves Himself strong.

We often treat suffering like a dodgeball game. Anytime anything hard comes at us, we jump out of the way. We spend our whole lives trying to avoid anything that will hurt or be hard. But there's a better kind of life—a deeper, more fulfilling kind of life—that isn't about avoiding every pain. It's about finding God faithful and powerful in the midst of whatever trials He allows.

There's something about our weakness that opens the flow of God's strength. When you admit your weakness in the midst of a trial, power comes into your life that you've never experienced before. When you see a hard thing coming, try saying, "I may not want this, but I know I'm going to see Christ work in my life in an incredible way." God never allows a thorn without providing sufficient grace and strength in our weakness. When Job was suffering terribly, God gave him grace in his weakness that allowed him to keep his eyes on his Savior. In the midst of his suffering Job declared, "I know that my Redeemer lives" (Job 19:25). God gave Job the strength he needed to endure his trial.

> When you admit your weakness in the midst of a trial, power comes into your life that you've never experienced before.

Are you currently trying to dodge the effects of a trial? ☐ **Yes** ☐ **No**

Sufficient grace is not just enough to survive but enough to have supernatural joy in the midst of anything God allows us to go through. In what areas do you need sufficient grace today? How are you depending on God to provide it?

All God's Kids Get Discipline

The road you walk through your trial is different from the dark road your non-Christian neighbors travel. They have no concept of what's going on in their lives, what it means, or where it's going. The fact that you are going through difficult days and you're not bitter but better and you love the Lord more—all of that is positive proof that you're a card-carrying member of the family of God. Hebrews 12:6 says, "The Lord disciplines the one he loves, and chastises every son whom he receives." If you're in a trial, see it as proof of God's love for you.

On the other hand, maybe you're thinking, *Everything is humming along in my life. No problems of any kind—money in the bank, no health crisis, kids are perfect, marriage is rocking!* That's not good news, because Hebrews 12:5-7 says all God's kids receive discipline. So if you're not going through any trials, you need to make sure you're really in the family.

If you are a child of God, discipline is coming your way; but so are a lot of amazing things. First John 3:1 says, "See what kind of love the Father has given to us, that we should be called children of God." As a child of God—

- you get hell canceled (amazing enough in itself!);
- you get heaven guaranteed;
- you get the Spirit of God as the deposit that the rest of God's blessings are coming;
- you get God's Word as a lifelong source of counsel, direction, wisdom, and truth;
- you get the assurance of the forgiveness of your sin;
- you get the glory of Christian fellowship.

Learn to see God's discipline as the blessing it is—as proof of His love for you.

Let me be loud and clear about this: God loves you. His eyes are on you every moment. You are never out of His thoughts. The Lord tells His people, "I have loved you with an everlasting love" (Jer. 31:3). Paul reminds us that nothing "will be able to separate us from the love of God in Christ Jesus our Lord" (Rom. 8:39). You didn't do anything to deserve His love; you don't do anything to maintain it. God has chosen to set His love on you, not because of who you are but because of who He is. He is your Father, and you are His child. Learn to see God's discipline as the blessing it is—as proof of His love for you.

Protect Your Joy

Endurance is critical to the Christian life. James 1 tells us that endurance is a characteristic God is trying to build into our lives. Perseverance and steadfastness enable us to keep our commitments. No matter how hard it seems, don't quit. You will develop endurance only by enduring.

Perseverance is the funnel through which all Christian virtue flows. If God can just get us not to be quitters, He can bring all other good things into our lives. If we won't quit our marriage, our kids, our job, our church, God will accomplish great things.

Instead of thinking the grass is greener somewhere else, we must believe, *This is where God has me. This is where I'm going to put down roots and plant my life and make a difference. If I stay here under the pressure, God can do amazing things in my life.* But we've got to be willing to commit for the long haul in order for God's trials to fulfill their purpose in our lives.

James tells us, "Blessed is the man who remains steadfast under trial, for when he has stood the test he will receive the crown of life" (1:12). The crown of life means the quality of life that God promises to those who love Him. If we endure, if we stand the test, there'll be a better life for us on the other side of this trial. Our best and most fruitful days are ahead. Our most God-glorifying days are ahead. God has a purpose in this trial, and if we hold up under it, we're going to receive the crown of life. It's a quality of life that comes to those who successfully pass the test—those who love Him. For some people it will be in eternity, but for most people it will begin at some point later in this life.

If we endure, if we stand the test, there'll be a better life for us on the other side of this trial.

Job, who graduated with honors from the school of suffering, expressed confidence that he would come out of his trial as gold. And Job 42 tells us that is exactly what happened. God rewarded Job's faithfulness and restored his prosperity, giving him wealth, livestock, and new sons and daughters. Best of all, Job got to know God more deeply than he had known Him before. He said:

> I had heard of you by the hearing of the ear,
> but now my eye sees you. *Job 42:5*

Protect your joy. Remain under the pressure. Don't let this trial steal what's ahead.

Think for a few moments about the statement "Perseverance is the funnel through which all Christian virtue flows." How have you found this to be true during a trial?

Why is remaining under a trial required for experiencing God's other blessings?

Identify a time when persevering through a trial resulted in joy.

A New Connection with the Lord

Recently, I was reading through a stack of my old journals that chronicle my relationship with God and all the things He has taught me over the years. I would have predicted that my sweetest times with the Lord were the times of greatest victory. But that wasn't the case. The frequency of entries and the intimacy of fellowship were much more apparent during times of hardship.

Why is that? Why does Christ seem so near during times of hardship? It's "the fellowship of His sufferings" that Philippians 3:10 (NKJV) talks about. Jesus knows about suffering; so when we suffer, we feel an affinity with Him. He draws near to us in hardship as in no other way. Hebrews 4:15 says, "We do not have a high priest who is unable to sympathize with our weaknesses."

First Peter 4:13 says, "Rejoice insofar as you share Christ's sufferings, that you may also rejoice and be glad when his glory is revealed." Twice in one verse, in the middle of a discussion on suffering, we are told to rejoice. But the second admonishment requires the first; if we rejoice in suffering, we can expect to rejoice in the revelation of Jesus' glory!

> **Suffering gives us a new understanding of Jesus and a new connection with Him.**

Why would we rejoice in suffering? Because we share in Christ's suffering. Suffering gives us a new understanding of Jesus and a new connection with Him. Some people say this verse refers to a future time when Christ's glory is revealed to the world. It could also mean we'll be glad when His glory is revealed in us here and now. We'll rejoice when we look in the mirror and see a different person, because the glory of Christ will be revealed through our lives. There's a closeness with the Lord that comes through trials that doesn't come any other way. Rejoice in the opportunity to show the superiority of a life lived in God.

Rejoicing is the external expression of joy. Record examples of times when you want to be intentional about rejoicing that you share in Christ's suffering.

Day 3

WHEN GOD DRAWS NEAR

Today's Scripture Focus
"He knows the way that I take;
when he has tried me, I shall come out as gold."
Job 23:10

Get your arms around this third really important truth:

God is never more present than when you are suffering.

The harder the trial, the closer He moves toward you. Are you feeling crushed today? God is rushing toward you to stand beside you and help you. Maybe you are not feeling close to God in the middle of your trial. Maybe you feel that God has abandoned you. It depends on what you think God's goals are. If you believe God exists to make you comfortable, you will find Him absent in your discomfort. If you believe God exists to make your life run smoothly, you will find Him absent when your life hits a rocky patch. If you believe God exists to make you happy, you will find Him absent when your heart is broken and your tears are flowing.

But if you believe God's goal is to make you holy, you will feel His arms around you in the center of your hardship. Through every intense, heart-wrenching moment of this trial, God's presence will become increasingly real.

> If you believe God's goal is to make you holy, you will feel His arms around you in the center of your hardship.

To have a right view of God, consider what He is doing in your trial. He is at work in your life the way a master craftsman works his art. You feel Him at work the way a house feels a carpenter, the way a sculpture feels a sculptor, the way a painting feels an artist—hammered, chiseled, and brushed. In Job's words, God is refining you like gold.

Check the phrase that describes your impression of God's nearness during your current trial.

☐ **Distant**   ☐ **Sporadic moments of intimacy**
☐ **Consistently near** ☐ **Never closer**
☐ **Other:**

If God has seemed distant, is it because you have held a mistaken view of God's goals for your trial?

Jesus Stands for You

Jesus Christ is an experienced sufferer. In case you hold in your mind a picture of an anemic, weak Jesus, replace it with this: Jesus has His PhD in suffering. He has suffered as no one else has suffered—for your sin and mine. Not only does Jesus identify with your suffering, but He is also present with you in your suffering. First Peter 4:14 says, "If you are insulted for the name of Christ, you are blessed, because the Spirit of glory and of God rests upon you."

You experience a unique intimacy with Christ when you suffer for Him. Think of Stephen in Acts 7 when he was giving up his life for Christ. As the crowd began to stone him, Stephen "gazed into heaven and saw the glory of God, and Jesus standing at the right hand of God" (v. 55). Why was Jesus standing? Hebrews states that after Jesus completed His redemptive mission to earth, "he sat down at the right hand of the Majesty on high" (1:3). Yet in this glimpse into glory, Stephen, at the moment of his greatest suffering, saw Jesus standing for him.

And it's not just emotional support. Jesus rose to honor, welcome, and identify with Stephen. As we've already seen, Paul described this new intimacy with Christ as "the fellowship of His sufferings" (Phil. 3:10, NASB). Believe by faith that in the middle of your trials, you are experiencing the fellowship of God's presence, which gives you new courage not to give up. *I'm not going to lose my faith, God help me. I'm going to keep on. I hate this world, but I'm longing for heaven. I'm going to serve Him until I get there.* In those moments of faith, God releases a wave of grace that rushes down on you.

> **Believe by faith that in the middle of your trials, you are experiencing the fellowship of God's presence.**

How do you keep this wave in motion? Keep your communication open with the Lord. I'm not talking about casual prayers over the shoulder. I mean on your face before God—a posture we've assumed too infrequently in our lives. And in that place the Lord will meet you. If you humble yourself, the Lord will be present with you. He is an experienced sufferer, fellowshipping with you.

God is never more present than when His children are suffering. Draw near.

Consider what it means to experience the fellowship of Christ's sufferings. In what circumstances have you felt that kind of connection with Jesus? How did the experience affect you?

God Listens

Do you think God really wants to talk to you? Do you think He really wants to hear what is on your heart? The answer is yes, He really does. God is an attentive counselor who listens to you in your trials. You understand this picture if you know what it's like to sit and talk to someone who really knows how to listen. They hear you. They get it. You can see in their eyes that they're tracking with you. Psalm 116:1-2 says:

> "I love the LORD, because he has heard
> my voice and my pleas for mercy.
> Because he inclined his ear to me …"

Picture your closest friend turning his ear to you. You cup your hand around your mouth and whisper your need. That's the picture.

God knows exactly what's going on in your life. He is aware of your needs and your heartaches and your worries about the future. God totally gets it. That one truth has inspired and comforted and ministered to God's people through thousands of years of history.

Not only is God listening to your prayer, but He will also give you wisdom about your trial if you ask Him for it. James 1:5 tells us, "If any of you lacks wisdom, let him ask God, who gives generously to all without reproach, and it will be given him." That phrase "without reproach" literally means God won't sink His teeth into you. God won't respond, "What? What are you asking Me that for?" He's not the impatient parent who doesn't have time for you or the irritable boss who snaps back. He's the attentive counselor who listens to you.

Read Psalm 62:8:

> "Trust in him at all times, O people;
> pour out your heart before him;
> God is a refuge for us."

Most of us have to admit there are times when we don't trust in God. List several of those times below and ask God to remind you during those times that trusting in Him invites His presence and aid.

God is an attentive counselor who listens to you in your trials.

For Your Good

I would have been a better-behaved kid if I could have been a parent first. Kids just don't understand what parents try to do for them. If you're a parent, don't you wish your kids could see that every action you take toward them, even imperfectly, is from love? Kids don't always get that. When I was an adolescent, I remember thinking my parents were so confused. Then I grew up, and as Mark Twain mused, I was amazed at how much they had learned.

I thought it was hard when I had to discipline my kids when they were young. Little kids are a quite a handful. When your kids get older and you must let them experience the consequences of their choices, they become quite a heartful. Especially when you can't step in and prevent the pain. You have to watch them suffer the cost of their decisions. For sure, heartful is harder than handful.

Are you in a trial as discipline from your loving Father? Do you feel His sadness that it had to come to this in order for you to learn? I don't want to get older and still be an adolescent Christian. I want to grow up in the Lord and trust my Heavenly Father even when I don't understand what He's doing. I want to believe the Lord is a lot smarter than I am. He gets it. His discipline is for my good.

Hebrews 12:7-8 tells the good but hard truth: "It is for discipline that you have to endure. God is treating you as sons. For what son is there whom his father does not discipline? If you are left without discipline, in which all have participated, then you are illegitimate children and not sons." Your Father loves you. Everything He allows is for your growth and your good. He sees the long picture even when you can't. It makes His heart sad when you don't understand that He lovingly draws near to you even in times of learning:

> "The LORD is near to the brokenhearted
> and saves the crushed in spirit." *Psalm 34:18*

In the middle of your trial, God is present as a loving Father who is disciplining His child.

When you think of God as Father, what aspects of your relationship with Him come to mind?

How do you respond to your Father's commitment to love you enough to discipline you?

In the middle of your trial, God is present as a loving Father who is disciplining His child.

God's Sufficient Grace

I'm not much of an original-language teacher, but once in a while I am rocked by some nuance of meaning I learn from the Bible's original language. I love the Greek word order of 2 Corinthians 12:9: "Sufficient for you is the grace of Me." That's an incredible promise!

Think for a moment about the regular place you meet with God. Is it a chair in your bedroom? Or at the kitchen table? Or as a father of five small children told me, is it the backseat of your car in the garage? I can picture the place where I met with God years ago in my dorm room at college; I can picture where I met with God in the apartment where we lived in seminary; I can picture the little blue love seat I used to sit on in our first house. I can picture my chair back at home right now where I meet with the Lord every day.

I find myself wondering, *How many times have I gotten up from that place and left God's sufficient grace there?* The Lord was there with me, holding out to me the grace for the trial I was going to face that day even as my mind was drifting off to my own plan. How many days did I run down the hall and off to my car and out to a busy day and leave Him sitting there with His sufficient grace?

"Sufficient for you is the grace of Me," God says. If I'm going to live by that sufficient grace, I'm not going to catch it falling from the sky as I run to my next appointment. I've got to go to the fountain and drink deeply. He is the One who quenches my thirst. He is the One who fills up what's missing. He is the One who satisfies my deepest longings. He is the One who brings and sustains a continuous revival in my life. He is all that to every thirsty soul who comes to Him for life and breath. When a trial threatens to overwhelm you, remember God's promise: "Sufficient for you is the grace of Me."

"Sufficient for you is the grace of Me."

Read James 4:8:

> "Draw near to God, and he will draw near to you."

In what ways are you drawing near to God during your trial?

How has God shown Himself to be grace for your trial?

Day 4
UNWAVERING SUBMISSION

Today's Scripture Focus
"He knows the way that I take;
when he has tried me, I shall come out as gold."
Job 23:10

Today we will study the final principle from our major passages of study:

*Until you embrace your trial in unwavering submission
to God, you will not reap the good.*

It really comes down to a choice: will you submit to God? Today's Scripture focus reminds us that Job had to make that choice just as we do. If anybody ever had a reason to give up on God, it was Job. After losing his children, his servants, and his wealth, he was afflicted with boils all over his body. He was in indescribable physical agony, and his family and friends deserted him (see Job 19:17-20). Yet he yielded to God's purposes, asking, "Shall we indeed accept good from God, and shall we not accept adversity?" (Job 2:10, NKJV). Job questioned why he was suffering, but he never wavered from submission to God.

If you are fighting God's discipline, you need to realize that you aren't going to win. To resist God in any way is just to delay failure. Sooner or later the flag will come down, the game will be over, and God will be the victor. Take a moment, figure out your chances of changing those odds, and get on God's side.

If you go against God in your trial, you will lose. You will get hurt. You will suffer the consequences. But if you submit to Him, you will reap the good. You will receive comfort and strength and wisdom and understanding. He will provide for your every need and fill your heart with happiness that is incomparable in this world. If you submit to God, you can win at things that matter. You can win in personal character. You can win in your family. You can win with your kids. You can win in your mind, your heart, and your soul. You can win for all eternity.

You may think you can never embrace your trial. God never said you could do anything good in your own strength. You need Him to do it through you. Embrace your trial in unwavering submission to God.

> **If you are fighting God's discipline, you need to realize that you aren't going to win.**

Where Victory Begins

If you're in a trial now, your constant choice is whether you will embrace or resist what God is doing in your life. Embracing God's purposes means you confess and live the reality that God is not asleep at the wheel. He is not AWOL. He is in control. He allowed this. You may wish that it wasn't so, that He could have prevented this trial. Yet He didn't. You have to embrace that He has allowed it and will use it for His purposes.

Resisting comes easier. We say, "No, not this," "No, not now," or "No, not me." We storm into (or out of) God's presence with our demands. Our pride blocks our view of God as long as we resist His purposes.

Complete these statements:

I resist God's discipline when I ...

I embrace God's discipline when I ...

I am aware of the weight of these words. I don't say them lightly. If you're in the water right now and the waves are crashing, you've got to get back on solid ground. But that's not going to happen until you embrace your trial.

Second Corinthians 12:10 says, "For the sake of Christ, then, I am content with weaknesses." The NIV says, "I delight in weaknesses." So many people don't get to this good place because they refuse to embrace the trial all the way to the end. They are like workers who never get paid, athletes who never win a game, or farmers who never make it to harvest time. Unless you embrace what God is doing with unwavering submission, you will not reap the good. Stay in the game. Don't resist. Submit to the Father's discipline.

Jesus Himself modeled this kind of victory in the garden of Gethsemane when He prayed, "Your will be done" (Matt. 26:42). Not My will, Father, but Your will. Not what I want, Father, but what You want. That's the essence of submission, and that's where victory begins.

> **Our pride blocks our view of God as long as we resist His purposes.**

Have you come to a place where you have submitted to God's discipline in your trial? If not, what do you think is holding you back?

Failure to Yield

Do you remember those yellow, triangular yield signs that used to be at intersections? Have you seen one lately? Unlikely. The traffic police had to make them all four-way stops. Why? Because nobody wanted to yield. Each person drove up to the corner and thought, *Clearly, I have the right of way, and clearly, he needs to yield.* We had an epidemic of traffic crashes because no one wanted to yield.

How good are you at yielding to God? Do you think, *Clearly, Lord, my way is better. This trial is taking my life in a direction that isn't in my plan, so I'm going to run the sign?* Have you ever stopped to think, *What if this trial is God's way of saying, "I want to take your life in a different direction"?*

Hebrews 12:9 asks, "Shall we not much more be subject to the Father of spirits and live?" In Greek, the original language, "be subject to" means *submit yourself,* indicating that you are the one who willingly makes this choice.

Remaining under the trial binds your heart to God.

God wants you to remain under the trial by your own choice, willingly yielding yourself to God so that "the testing of your faith produces steadfastness" (Jas. 1:3). Remaining under the trial binds your heart to God. It will make you irreversibly devoted and committed to Jesus Christ.

Yielding doesn't come easily in a culture of individualism. We like to think we can do things on our own, but the only way through a trial is to yield to God. If you haven't submitted your trial to Him, are you ready to pray the following? "This isn't where I thought my life would be today, but I'm going to yield. I'm stopping, God. You go. I'm going to fall in behind You." Describe the way you are going to let God have His way and yield to His purposes.

Making It Stick

How do you make it stick? How do you make your commitment to submit to God withstand the beating of the wind and waves of adversity? If you're like me, sometime in the past you've given something to God only to wake up the next day with it back in your hands. *I gave this to God. What's it doing back here?*

One day I surrender to God that difficult something that threatens to take me under. "Here it is, God. Take it. Help me." The next day—without even realizing it—I'm back in charge again. I'm nurturing my own set of rights and privileges. So back on my knees I go, submitting again to God. "Here I am again, God. My life is Yours. Not me but You."

So how do you remain in a state of submission? I have found that the only way to maintain my submission to God is through believing prayer. Back on my knees, I give it back to God. I have to keep giving it back until I've broken the habit of taking it back.

James 1:6-8 says a doubting Christian is "like a wave of the sea that is driven and tossed by the wind. For that person must not suppose that he will receive anything from the Lord; he is a double-minded man, unstable in all his ways." The opposite of doubt is faith. You stand on solid rock when the storm beats you from all sides. Believing prayer says, "Here I am again, God. I'm standing here on this rock. Here in this trial I'm standing still and strong."

If you're in a trial now, you need to stand on that rock and pray as you've never prayed before. You know you need God's sustaining grace. Surrender once again to God. Get up from your work, step aside from whatever you're doing, and give your burden to the Lord this moment, day by day, and week by week. You can maintain your submission to God only through believing prayer.

Embrace your trial in unwavering submission to God by coming back to the throne of grace again and again. There you are always welcome: "Let us then with confidence draw near to the throne of grace, that we may receive mercy and find grace to help in time of need" (Heb. 4:16).

How do you think prayer helps you maintain your submission to God during a trial?

> You can maintain your submission to God only through believing prayer.

Check the word that best describes your prayer life since your trial began.

- ☐ **Sporadic**
- ☐ **Constant**
- ☐ **Once a day**
- ☐ **Occasional**
- ☐ **When in trouble**
- ☐ **Other:**

You're Not Going Under

There is nothing good that God brings into your life by way of transformation that He doesn't bring through the funnel of perseverance. If God can develop perseverance in your life, He can truly make you what He wants you to be.

First Peter 4:19 encourages us, "Let those who suffer according to God's will entrust their souls to a faithful Creator while doing good." Did you hear what you're supposed to do? Entrust your soul to your faithful Creator. God is faithful to you. In the middle of it all, He tells you to entrust yourself to His care.

God knows you better than you know yourself. You're not going to lose it; you're going to be OK. You don't know what you are capable of when you're resting in God's strength and not your own. You're going to get through this if you fully submit to Him. It's not going to last forever, and you will get through it because God is faithful.

Reassure yourself, *I'm not going under.* You can keep going for another day, another week because God is producing staying power in you. The ability to remain in that marriage—as hard as it is. The ability to remain in that job—as hard as it is. The ability to stick with it in that difficult circumstance—no matter what. The good won't come if you quit. God can develop every characteristic of Christ in your life if He can just teach you to persevere through your trial.

Indicate the way you feel about your trial at this point.

- ☐ **Going under**
- ☐ **On solid rock**
- ☐ **Other:**

Pray and entrust your soul to your faithful Creator, expressing your confidence that He will see you through this trial.

God is faithful.

Day 5

GO FOR THE GOLD

Today's Scripture Focus

"He knows the way that I take;
when he has tried me, I shall come out as gold."
Job 23:10

We began this week's study with an overview of the ancient process of refining gold (p. 133). It remains unchanged today. Likewise, God is still using the same approach He has always used with people. We come to Him as ore; He refines us into gold. As Job's life demonstrates, the furnace God employs still includes the heat, pressure, and pain of trials. We have spent the past four days chewing on four essential, hope-preserving truths that God has revealed about Himself and His reasons for allowing us to experience hard times:

Every trial you face is allowed by God for your ultimate good.

Your trial doesn't need to steal your joy.

God is never more present than when you are suffering.

*Until you embrace your trial in unwavering submission to God,
you will not reap the good.*

In the previous list, underline the truth you have studied this week that encourages you most in your present struggle with a trial.

Job's words in this week's Scripture focus say it all. As Job endured his trial, he was intent on remaining faithful to God. He wasn't sure why he was suffering, but he was sure that God knew what he was going through and would bring good from it. Job's words carry an indelible promise that he would be refined as gold.

God always has a purpose for your suffering. While life on this side of eternity lasts, God's refining process continues. He knows exactly what kind of furnace you are in today. He allowed it. And when the particular impurities and slag have been removed, other trials will come.

While life on this side of eternity lasts, God's refining process continues.

One crucial difference between you and gold ore is that you know what's happening. Gold melts; you resist. Gold releases its impurities under heat; you hang on to yours. Gold remains silent; you do not. Your spirit and your mouth cry out your confusion and frustration. But if you remain under, if you learn to submit to the Refiner's fire, the results will be amazing. You will come out as gold.

I want to complete our study together by encouraging you to pray the following prayer. Read it twice, once to make it your own, then again to give it to your Heavenly Father.

Lord, I'm staying right here. I'm not going anywhere. I'm not looking for a way out. I'm remaining right here under the pressure of Your refining work.

And I yield. As best as I know how, God, I'm not fighting You. I'm not angry with You. I'm confused sometimes. I'm perplexed. I'm sad. But I'm not angry. I trust You to use this trial as Your loving training to change my conduct and my character.

I'm not going to quit, Lord. By Your grace and in Your strength, I'm going to keep doing the things You've called me to do. I'm going to hold on to You, believing that Your grace is sufficient. I'm going to get closer to You and go deeper with You as You draw near to me in my suffering.

I'm embracing this trial. I believe Your promises that You will bring good in my life through this trial. I'm treasuring these things in my heart, and I'm committing to You once again here and now, God, that in Your sufficient grace I'm going forward. Give me joy. Teach me perseverance. Turn these trials to gold in my life. I'm waiting to see it. My hope is in You.

In Jesus' name, for His glory, amen.

Two Ways to Earn Credit
for Studying LifeWay Christian Resources Material

CHRISTIAN GROWTH STUDY PLAN

CONTACT INFORMATION:
Christian Growth Study Plan
One LifeWay Plaza, MSN 117
Nashville, TN 37234
CGSP info line 1-800-968-5519
www.lifeway.com/CGSP
To order resources 1-800-458-2772

Christian Growth Study Plan resources are available for course credit for personal growth and church leadership training.

Courses are designed as plans for personal spiritual growth and for training current and future church leaders. To receive credit, complete the book, material, or activity. Respond to the learning activities or attend group sessions, when applicable, and show your work to your pastor, staff member, or church leader. Then go to *www.lifeway.com/CGSP,* or call the toll-free number for instructions for receiving credit and your certificate of completion.

For information about studies in the Christian Growth Study Plan, refer to the current catalog online at the CGSP Web address. This program and certificate are free LifeWay services to you.

Need a CEU?

CONTACT INFORMATION:
CEU Coordinator
One LifeWay Plaza, MSN 150
Nashville, TN 37234
Info line 1-800-968-5519
www.lifeway.com/CEU

Receive Continuing Education Units (CEUs) when you complete group Bible studies by your favorite LifeWay authors.

Some studies are approved by the Association of Christian Schools International (ACSI) for CEU credits. Do you need to renew your Christian school teaching certificate? Gather a group of teachers or neighbors and complete one of the approved studies. Then go to *www.lifeway.com/CEU* to submit a request form or to find a list of ACSI-approved LifeWay studies and conferences. Book studies must be completed in a group setting. Online courses approved for ACSI credit are also noted on the course list. The administrative cost of each CEU certificate is only $10 per course.

LifeWay
Biblical Solutions for Life

OTHER STUDIES BY
JAMES MACDONALD

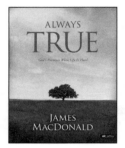

Always True: God's Promises When Life Is Hard

This study reveals God as the great Promise Keeper who loves making promises to His children and who always keeps those promises. James MacDonald explores five key promises from Scripture and five ways believers can respond to the promises by faith. Six sessions.

Leader Kit 005274675 • Member Book 005371573

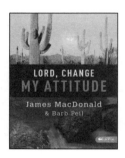

Lord, Change My Attitude

Based on the Israelites' journey out of Egypt, this study shows how attitudes can affect whether someone stays in the wilderness with negative attitudes or enjoys the blessings of the promised land with God-honoring attitudes. Eleven sessions.

Leader Kit 005097385 • Member Book 005035039

Gripped by the Greatness of God

Based on key teachings from the Book of Isaiah, this study challenges believers to be gripped by God's greatness and to respond to God in worship with renewed zeal, passion, and heartfelt excitement. Eight sessions.

Leader Kit 001288992 • Member Book 001288990

Downpour: He Will Come to Us like the Rain

James MacDonald leads Christians to take the personal steps they need to return to the Lord and experience spiritual renewal and victory. Member book includes a music CD of songs related to the topic. Twelve sessions.

Leader Kit 001303831 • Member Book 001303830

To purchase these resources, write to LifeWay Church Resources Customer Service; One LifeWay Plaza; Nashville, TN 37234-0113; fax (615) 251-5933; e-mail *orderentry@lifeway.com;* phone toll free (800) 458-2772; order online at *www.lifeway.com;* or visit the LifeWay Christian Store serving you.